Reform Yourself!

SHAUN MCAFEE

REFORM
YOURSELF!

HOW TO PRAY, FIND PEACE, AND GROW IN FAITH
WITH THE SAINTS OF THE COUNTER-REFORMATION

Foreword by Paul Thigpen

Catholic
Answers
Press

Published by Catholic Answers, Inc.
2020 Gillespie Way
El Cajon, California 92020
888-291-8000 orders
619-387-0042 fax
www.catholic.com

Printed in the United States of America

ISBN 978-1-68357-054-7
       978-1-68357-055-4 Kindle
       978-1-68357-056-1 ePub

To you, the reader.
You are the Church.

Contents

Foreword

More than thirty years ago, I was a Protestant pastor working my way through a Ph.D. program in Church History at a Methodist university. The process was an essential factor in my eventually becoming Catholic. As Blessed John Henry Newman famously observed, "To be deep in history is to cease to be Protestant."

As I studied, I learned almost daily not only how much I didn't know, but also how much of what I thought I knew was actually untrue.

One of the great surprises awaiting me when I studied what Church historians call the "Reformation Period" was the Catholic movement known as the Counter-Reformation. Many prefer to call it the *Catholic Reformation*, and for good reason: it was not just a reaction, a "counter," to the Protestant revolt. The spirit of genuine reform within the Catholic Church, as opposed to her attempted reform through fragmentation, long preceded Martin Luther's posting of the Ninety-Five Theses on October 31, 1517—the episode commonly considered the birth of the Protestant movement.

This year marks the 500th anniversary of that event. Understandably, Protestants around the world are celebrating this year as a spiritual milestone. Meanwhile, many Catholics are seeking a better understanding of the situation that provoked Luther's action and its earth-shaking consequences. In their search for such understanding, and to learn how the Catholic Church responded and how its response can be spiritually fruitful even today, they would do well to read this book.

The sixteenth-century Church was in dire need of reform; few would challenge that observation. Moral decadence and corruption abounded at every level: from the infamous "Renaissance popes" to princely bishops, from sexually active and doctrinally ignorant priests to a laity that was often—not surprisingly—clueless and confused by such failed leadership. Of course, there were good Catholics to be found in every place. But the lax and the loathsome seemed immovably entrenched, and all too often they were the ones in charge.

In the midst of this spiritual darkness, God sent a number of heroic men and women to bring about authentic reform. They faced considerable opposition—as did the leaders who, after Luther's movement found numerous followers, sought to reclaim those who had been lost to the Church. These bold, brave souls risked more than we can imagine to fulfill their missions of reform and reclamation, often laying their lives on the line to defend the Faith and to seek out those who had wandered away.

In these pages you'll read about ten of these genuine spiritual heroes and what they have to teach us today. Their stories should stir us with admiration for their exceptional holiness, wisdom, courage, and perseverance—and often a fine sense of humor as well. But the author has given us much more than simple biography; he connects these stories to our everyday work of *self*-reform, of ongoing conversion, as well as to our baptismal call to explain and defend the Faith. Always, he approaches these saints with an essential question in mind: *What can we learn from their example?*

I trust this book will find a wide audience. My hope is that readers will respond eagerly to the challenges it issues through its perceptive look at ten extraordinary saints with profound lessons for ordinary Catholics.

Paul Thigpen, Ph.D.
Kennesaw, Georgia

Acknowledgments

When I was in the seventh grade my English teacher assigned the class to write a short story. I quickly got out my mechanical pencil and a paper, put my name and date at the top right corner, and raised my hand to ask, "What should I put as the title?"

I've always remembered her remark: "Why don't you write it first and then choose a title?" She was right, and that advice has served me well as an author: work first, always. It's a mantra I've applied to many aspects of my life, and a similar initiative was applied to this book. I wish to thank and acknowledge the team of professionals at Catholic Answers for finding the right niche for this book from content, to title, to the cover art. It was not what any of us had in mind from the beginning, but it is now a head-turning book from every angle and chapter. Thank you, sincerely, Todd Aglialoro, Tim Ryland, Jon Sorensen, and the rest of the team who contributed to the development of this book.

I wish secondly to acknowledge and thank my wife for her continual support of my writing: seemingly endless book buying, providing me with time to write on early mornings and late nights, and encouragement throughout the process. I could not have done this without you. Thank you, Jessica, my love.

There's another contributing acknowledgement I would like to make and that is about the dedication. Like the title, this is one of the last things I finalize on a book. The morning I had to make a decision. I asked my wife, "Whom should I dedicate the book to?"

She provided a resoundingly fresh answer: "Who did you think of the most when you were writing the book?" The answer was easy: *you, the readers*. From the very beginning, and with each tippy-tap as I punched the keys, I wanted every word to be beneficial to the reader. I wanted to create a book that doesn't just help people learn *about saints*, but to learn *from saints*. What you have in your hands is a book made for you, to give you a courageous faith and a desire to persistently reform yourself, because you are the Church.

Introduction

It is said that if you want to become a saint, you must read the saints. But I say, if you want to become a saint, you must do more than read: you must *study* the saints! You must read the saints in detail, analyzing them to the degree to which you come to know your own friends and family, taking an interest in every detail of their characters. To know these saints, we must devote ourselves to them. Only when we do this can we become like them.

The first question to ask yourself, then, is: *What saints should I study?* Well, naturally, that depends. It depends on what sort of saint you want to become. Do you enjoy study and scholarship? Might you enjoy the work of preaching? Missionaries and service to others? If you want to become a saint of great intellect, you must study the academic saints: Augustine, Aquinas, Edith Stein, and others. To become a saint of great virtue you must study the virtuous saints: John Paul II, Maximilian Kolbe, Thérèse of Lisieux, Mary of Egypt, Teresa of Calcutta. There are those who are deeply encouraged by the spiritual saints, the mystics, and saints who have performed astonishing miracles. If you want to imitate these saints, you must surround yourself with them as friends.

You should ask yourself what your primary vocation *already is*. A mother or father would do well to study the lives of those saints who had children. A priest would be smart to study the lives of the great pastors of souls. Even popes should study former popes and the bishops they admire. If you are already involved in a particular vocation—as many of us are—you have an obligation to faithfully live out that vocation. This cloud of witnesses, the saints, will help you do both!

There's no end to the saints we can study, nor the saints we *should* study. Becoming a saint, though, is never about us. Ideally, rather than focus on a specific dynamic or interest of our own, we should concentrate on becoming vessels of the Holy Spirit that are capable of being used for whatever the times of the Church demand of us.

During the time of the Reformation (1517-1648), the Church had an unprecedented need of men and women of heroic virtue. The Faith, which had withstood persecution in its infancy, destruction from within through various heresies later, and moral corruption from popes, cardinals, and bishops who placed their self-interest and immorality above the demands of their office, was in dire straits. The Church was in a dark place, perhaps the darkest it has ever endured. It needed exceedingly honorable saints.

Many date the beginning of the Reformation to 1517, when Martin Luther is said to have nailed his Ninety-Five Theses to the doors of the Wittenberg Castle Church. This condemnation of Catholic practices encouraged many to turn from their Church and abandon the Faith of their fathers, and it lit the European landscape in religious and idealistic wildfire. What could have been a complete implosion of Mother Church was saved by the courageous and judicious acts of the saints of the Counter-Reformation.

The Church was in need of reform in nearly every way: moral, catechetical, liturgical, ecumenical, educational, formational, and the saints who made such an impact on the Church in the sixteenth century were as diverse. Pius V, through his shrewd and strict leadership, was able to restructure and reorganize educational institutions and institutes of priestly formation. Ignatius of Loyola, a military officer, sparked interest in a new religious order that made decisive rectifications in all places where Protestant ideas had advanced. Simpler saints like Aloysius Gonzaga, a mere boy, had such unrivaled piety that he was able to convict the most powerful clergy and laymen. The heroes of the Counter-Reformation came from all walks of life and made considerably different marks on this critical period in Church history.

Selected for their many achievements and their enduring legacy, the ten saints in this book aren't the only saints of the Counter-Reformation, but they are the ones we should study and emulate as especially useful models and guides in the ongoing work of *self-reform* in which we're all engaged: the work of growing in holiness. So, this book is not intended as a biographical survey of the lives of these saints, but as a manual for imitating these saints in order to become purer vessels of the Holy Spirit. I hope it will be a road map for becoming a true reformer of your own soul.

Chapter 1

St. Francis de Sales
The Apologist Next Door

August 21, 1567–December 28, 1622
Feast Day: January 24

"Be who you are and be that well."

On a wintry night, a young student carries books back to his residence after a long day of studying law and literature in Padua. He has a French accent and he comes from an influential family. The twenty-year-old is smarter and wittier than his classmates, and more handsome, too. Perceiving him to be a threat, a gang of his classmates have arranged an ambush, and as they wait in their positions, the young man studies his surroundings. As quick and studied with a sword as he is with his books, the young man pounces on the gang and sends them into a confused frenzy. Without drawing blood, at once they are on their knees invoking apology and praying for his mercy. Temperate, he forgives them and lets them go without a word. The expression on his face tells them everything they need to know.

He's Francis de Sales, who would one day become the "Gentle Saint," but he wasn't a doormat. He understood the proper measure of justice and the application of law, while also having a heart of mercy and love for his enemies and those of the Church. In his letters to heretics, he always refers to them as "friend," and in each of these apologetic debates he provided supremely persuasive arguments connecting faith and reason.

In his lifetime he converted tens of thousands of Calvinist adherents, founded a religious order, and wrote several thousand letters and tracts on the Faith. His life was full of accomplishments, and yet he maintained a neighborly familiarity, and always was the leader a person could to go at any time, for any reason. The Counter-Reformation needed good apologists and good counselors of profound holiness, and that is just the sort of reformer that St. Francis de Sales was.

Apostolic Charm

The motto of the bishop of Geneva and world-famous apologist was "Ask for nothing, refuse nothing," and he was the total embodiment of his personal philosophy. No matter the occasion, he tossed aside his own ambitions and projects both for the most menial task in service of the lowest person, and the most daunting and life-threatening tasks of popes and kings. Despite his repute, he was a very approachable person. In combination with his intellect and ability to gather apologetics resources to refute and persuade dissenters, perhaps it was this "saint next door" quality that made him so effective.

Francis de Sales came from nobility and had rank, but he was not a lifelong student of dogma or apologetics. He became brilliant at converting others to the Catholic faith when he used the arguments provided by scholars like Robert Bellarmine, Thomas Aquinas, and Boethius. He utilized their materials to create and print clever tracts that he distributed in parishes and slipped under doors at night. Like a modern blogger, he didn't have to reinvent the wheel with apologetics and theology: he simply had to simplify and disseminate the words of other scholars. He let them do the heavy lifting while he passed on their arguments to the masses. It helped that he was versed in logic and debate from his studies in law, but his tactic was not to create novel arguments but to use what already worked for the betterment of the kingdom. It's worth noting that he is the patron saint of the Catholic press, not the patron saint of Catholic writers or apologists. That's because he understood the value of effective communication, using new technologies to reach and convert thousands who dissented from the Catholic faith, and educate thousands more who desired orthodoxy. It is instructive to be reminded that his most popular writings are devotionals and guides for the spiritual and religious, not works of apologetics or exegeses on Holy Writ.

Francis was an apologist people could go to with any question. What made him so effective was that he wasn't interested in winning arguments for himself, but in winning souls for Christ. He was truly a friend and counselor at heart. Understanding the relationship between apologetics and being a friend and counselor is the key to unlocking the reason people convert: reason and relationships. It's a fact that there's always a central issue or stumbling block that prevents others from joining the Catholic faith. For some, it's the Blessed Virgin Mary. For others, it's the pope. Whatever the issue, these people need *reasons*, but they also need *relationships*. Few people will convert to an entirely new religion without surety that they will receive moral support during their transition and friendships that might last long after. They might convert in their heads, but they will lose heart after a time if they don't have these. The same can be said for those who convert in the interest of their relationships, but sacrifice their mental stumbling blocks. These people will enjoy their friendship or marriage for a time, but there will always remain the elephant in the room or the disinterest in attending Mass and support-ing the catechesis of their children. In the end, people need reason and good apologetics, as well as the strengthening support of friends and good counsel. Francis de Sales was the epitome of this combination.

The two universal constants in our life are that we all know non-Catholics and that we are called to evangelize. Evangelization *does* involve being an apologist. Our first pope made this clear: "Always be ready to give an explana-tion to anyone who asks you for a reason for your hope" (1 Pet. 3:15, NABRE). We don't need to be published authors and respected speakers to be good apologists and counselors, (though defending the Faith may involve both writing and speaking). Evangelization, above all, includes being willing to be a friend and a counselor. We will recall Francis's words of counsel, and use his supreme example of nurturing rela-tionships in order to help us become "next-door" apologists.

Powerful Communicator

Apologists principally defend the Faith in speaking and in writing. Now, many who believe they are good writers of-ten hate public speaking, or are not confident when asked a question in the spur of a moment. They prefer to gather their thoughts and put them to paper over time. Others don't shy from an oral challenge but are intimidated by the task of writ-ing, seeing it as an impossible mountain of work and puzzle-piecing. All of us who want to defend the Faith should, like Francis de Sales, strive to be effective in both writing and speech. A defense may be required of us in an email, or over dinner, on the golf course, in a social media post, on a blog, or in line at the supermarket. Whether the task is big or small, the apologist should always be ready.

Francis de Sales was *always ready.* This preparedness came over a period of time. Yes, he had a tremendous intellect, but his knowledge was not infused. Nobody is born a saint and nobody is born a Doctor of the Church. Francis worked for a lifetime to become both. Yet, studious and devoted as he was, his knowledge was nothing without his ability to communicate it effectively, which is precisely what we must learn in order to be great counter-reformers ourselves. Those who are scared of public speaking or who dread the clickety-clack of their keyboard should make Francis their model. Let's discuss a few of the techniques we can learn to be better communicators.

If you want to write more, read more. There's no getting around this. The avid reader becomes a better writer. Reading expands our vocabularies and habituates our minds to the artful expression of ideas. For an apologist, moreover, wide reading exposes us to the best of arguments and the worst of arguments, the oldest of opinions and the newest of opinions, the most ancient heresies and the most novel. Francis was able to unravel every sort of argument and idea because he was heavily read. Indeed, he said little of the books he wrote, but always promoted those he read and trusted.

If you want to write better, read better. Have you ever found yourself halfway down a page with no clue what you just read? Have you ever found yourself re-reading a paragraph several times while your mind is somewhere else? Reading is a skill, too, one that requires focus and practice. Here's four of the best recommendations for improving this skill:

1. *Read at a pace that is sufficient for your level of study.* Reading a math textbook or the *Summa Theologiae* should be much slower than reading a comic or a tract, so take your time based on the level of study required.

2. *Keep notes.* Francis, like Thomas Aquinas and other scholarly saints, was known to keep copious notes in the margins of his personal books. Create a system that marks and cross-references important ideas, and don't be afraid to jot down your own personal reminders and annotations in the white space (or using the notes app on your e-reader!).

3. *Make use of reference guides, compendiums, and commentaries.* Reading primary sources is critical, but nobody becomes an expert after reading Augustine's *De Trinitate once.* Also take advantage of the resources of theologians and teachers who are experts in their subject.

4. *Try to enjoy what you read.* If you enjoy what you're reading, chances are very good that you'll retain more, and retain it longer. When selecting books to read, remember to get the ones that keep you engaged and challenged.

Remember that everyone has a different learning curve, and it doesn't all happen overnight—or in a week or month or year. Becoming a better reader and writer is a *lifestyle.*

The bishop of Geneva was a model of another indispensable writing virtue: brevity. He took seriously the advice of his namesake, St. Francis of Assisi, who instructed members of his order to be brief in their preaching, quoting St. Paul to the Romans: "For he shall finish his word, and cut it short in justice; because a short word shall the Lord make upon the earth" (9:28).

In a letter to another bishop, de Sales writes:

Believe me, I speak from experience, the more you say the less will be remembered and the less will your hearers profit. By overloading their memory you can cause it to break down, as lamps are put out by too much oil and plants are killed by too much watering. [An author] can have no greater fault than lengthiness. Say little, but say it well and to the purpose.[1]

This is great advice for those wanting to improve the effectiveness of their writing, and Francis applies the same to oral instruction from the pulpit or the stage.

What should be the content of the writing of those who wish to defend the Faith effectively? Francis offers another pithy bit of saintly wisdom:

> I have always maintained that whoever preaches with love, preaches sufficiently against heresy, although he may not utter a word of controversy. During all these years that God has called me to preach his word to the people, I have remarked that practical sermons, where the subject is treated with zeal and devotion, are so many burning coals cast upon the head of Protestants who hear them; and they are always pleased and edified by them, and are thereby rendered more docile and reasonable when we confer with them on disputed points. This is not my opinion only, but is that of the most celebrated preachers I know. They all agree that the pulpit ought not to be a battleground of controversy, and that we must demolish more than we build up if we attempt more than a passing allusion to it.[2]

He gave this advice to a brother bishop who was desperate to find the right approach to converting a prominent and bothersome Protestant in his diocese. This was the same tactic Francis used in his meetings with the duke of Lesdiguières, who had fallen away to Calvinism and never given any sign of returning to Catholicism, but was intrigued enough by the bishop of Geneva that they met on a couple of occasions. In the years that followed, Francis's pithy arguments stewed in his mind and eventually he and many of his soldiers were reconciled to the Church.

Writing is important. It's the universal art. But speech is the more common way an apologist communicates. Everyone speaks, but the good speaker must be heard. Many speakers are heard, but the apologist is *understood*.

Francis de Sales didn't have a teleprompter; he had his memory. He didn't have a stage manager dictating his transitions in an earpiece; he had his intellect and his intuition. He didn't have a high-tech sound system; he used his diaphragm and exploited acoustics. Now, you might never be asked to speak to a crowd, but you will almost certainly be called upon to defend the Faith on a smaller scale: with friends, relatives, door-to-door missionaries, and so on. When you do so, here are some key things that Francis de Sales can teach you:

- *Be brief.* When de Sales was a younger priest he was confronted after Mass for giving long-winded homilies. After the productive exchange, Francis realized he didn't need to *say a lot* to *communicate a lot*, and thus he committed to brief but striking homilies.

- *Think quickly, but don't speak quickly.* The proverb says, "The mind of the righteous ponders how to answer, but the mouth of the wicked pours out evil things" (Prov. 15:38), and it is absolutely correct. There's a powerful temptation to deliver an answer immediately with the fear of not sounding confident, studied, or prepared. Ignore those temptations and take your time. Draw a deep breath, pause, and put together the best answer you can. Eventually, you'll be able to answer quicker, but until then never answer quicker than the answer deserves.

- *Ask questions.* It's very important to have answers, but there are times when, to give the best answer, you need to ask more questions. Doing this will help you get to the real issue, problem, or disagreement. Asking questions can sometimes reveal flaws in the logic or selective judgment of your inquirer.

- *If you want to speak better, listen better.* Communicating is a two-way road, and you're going to build rapport with your listener if you let him talk while *actively* listening to him. A good listener presents positive body language, shows interest, asks questions, displays concern, and demonstrates respect for differing opinions.

Francis's own father recognized the simple power of his communication style, if in a backhanded way. Francis relays the story to us:

My father, hearing the bell ring for devotions, would inquire: "Who is going to preach?" and the reply was always: "Who should it be but your son, the provost?" This annoyed him greatly, so much so that he remonstrated with me. "Look here, provost," he said, "you preach too much too often; you make yourself too cheap. And then your sermons!—*grand Dieu!* no Latin, no Greek, no learned questions. Your language is so simple and unstudied, a child could understand it."[3]

When all else fails... There will be times when you don't have the answers. When this happens, know where to direct people. You don't have to be the last word; often you will do more good by putting people in touch with other resources than you can do with your own knowledge alone.

Friend and Counselor

Francis de Sales had a reputation for apologetics throughout the Christian world. Relatively few, however, knew him as his close companions and spiritual subjects knew him: as a friend and counselor. He was a true shepherd of souls. His prolific writing contained a great deal of spiritual direction. Through correspondence, personal meetings and conversations, short letters and book-length exhortations, Francis went out of his way to give everyone what they needed to get to heaven. He is the "apologist next door" because he made himself accessible for a quick question on a front porch in his diocese, or in an abandoned parish in Calvinist territory. Francis reminds us that "A holy friendship is nigh indispensable for the welfare of souls."[4]

Being a friend and counselor is a special gift and an important responsibility, requiring a high level of gentleness, trust, and persuasiveness. Imitating Francis de Sales means being wise and smart, but also realizing we are each called to evangelize as friends of good counsel.

Francis is often called "the gentle saint" and it's an accurate moniker. Even when he was young and carried a sword, he understood that the more powerful weapon was his tongue. He would escape trouble with humor, and by his wit he led others to become converts and close friends. It was he who coined the expression, "One can catch more flies with a spoonful of honey than with a hundred barrels of vinegar."[5] His ability to calm an escalating situation was not only imperative to his success as an apologist, but also as a friend and counselor. We can only imagine the hundreds of times his advice caused discomfort, or his correction caused outbursts. But over time he learned that his direction was better received when he was gentle. Francis likely read the biblical proverbs about the tongue many times in prayer: "A soft answer turns away wrath, but a harsh word stirs up anger" (Prov. 15:1) and "A gentle tongue is a tree of life, but perverseness in it breaks the spirit" (Prov. 15:4).

When we talk to others it should always be with respect for their dignity. This other person may be a mean boss, a stubborn child, or a recalcitrant heretic, but the words of Francis apply to all: "The remonstrances of a father given gently and affectionately have much more power to correct the child than those which are given angrily wrathfully."[6] "One kind word wins more willing service than a hundred harsh orders or stern reproofs."[7] "Anger is quieted by a gentle word just as fire is quenched by water."[8] Francis believed that everyone deserves this saintly gentleness, and he offers a few key precepts we must adopt to do so.

When correcting or counseling, we should *be cogent.* We should give clear instructions and offer alternatives persuasively. When we speak, Francis advises us, "Let your speech be gentle, frank, sincere, straightforward, candid, and faithful."[9] In other words, we should let there be no mistake about our intention and our message. That doesn't mean we should go out of our way to be shockingly blunt. It is always best—to the best of our abilities—to exercise communication that is open, honest, but tactful. As Francis tells us, sometimes winning people over involves more love than fact-telling: "We must fight back with affection and not with reason."[10]

Early in his missionary journeys in Chablais, where militant Calvinists threatened the lives of Catholics, Francis was chided for his loving manner toward them. Though he hated heresy, he always loved the heretic. His fellow missionaries sometimes would reproach him, urging him to be harsher and more strident. To such scolding he responded:

> Never have I been too severe or rigorous with heretics that I have not had reason to regret my austerity. Instead of doing good, bitter words and invectives only infuriate and make them more obstinate. I have had the happiness of converting a few heretics but I have done so with kindness and gentleness. Love and affection have a greater empire over souls than harshness and severity. Love is more powerful than the strongest of arguments, the most convincing of reasons.[11]

Sometimes words, even loving words, aren't the best option, but *silence* is. Francis gave this advice to St. Jane Francis de Chantal:

> Do not speak quickly, answer slowly, humbly and gently, and let your silence often speak for you. Greatly support and make allowances for others with great kindness of heart. Do not dwell on contradictions and troubles; look only on God and submit yourself completely to his Divine will. Do everything for God, turning your eyes and your heart always toward him.[12]

St. Francis is not saying never to speak up. He's saying to choose silence first as a matter of good measure; that we must have the good judgment to decide when to speak up and when to relax our tongue. Being silent is less about not having something to say and more about knowing the *right thing* to say but waiting to say it at the *right time*. "Mere silence is not wisdom, for wisdom consists of knowing when and how to speak and when and where to keep silent," says our gentle saint.[13] Listening to an adversarial opinion is a highly beneficial tactic, but there is a right time and place for correction. If someone preaches a heretical idea or lies about the character of another, Francis tell us, "It is a sovereign remedy against lying to unsay the lie on the spot."[14]

When giving advice and guidance, choose *authenticity.* Don't be a hypocrite or you'll instantly lose rapport and respect. Being a good counselor does require giving frequent advice, but it is more about always being a stalwart example. Before giving counsel to another, be sure that you are not in flaming contradiction to that advice and also ensure that you are fair in your measure. Francis says, "Do not require more from others than from yourself"[15] and, "Be more indulgent toward others and more disciplinary with yourself."[16]

In addition to being authentic and fair, when giving counsel and instructions it is a good idea to *adapt such guidance* to the needs and abilities of that person. Francis tells us, "Remember that the practice of devotion must be adapted to the strength, the employment, and the duties of each one in particular."[17] Francis withheld penances from some who didn't need them and withheld praise from others who were too full of their own pride, and in this way he governed and pastored his flock with brilliant judgment. Along these lines, become familiar with the saints who may better inspire and intercede on behalf of your friend. Our saint advises us to "choose some particular saints whose lives you can best appreciate and imitate, and in whose intercession you may have a particular confidence."[18]

Lastly, gentle counselors must remember that the *journey to holiness is not made overnight.* "We must strive not to practice many exercises at once, or the enemy often tries to make us undertake many designs, to the end that, overwhelmed with the multiplicity of business, we may accomplish nothing."[19]

You can't be friends with everyone. Remember when doing apologetics and evangelization that, when you fail, it was not because you didn't say the perfect words or that you didn't love that person enough. Even Jesus, who totally and perfectly understood the human heart, could not win over his enemies and conspirators. Francis assures us, "When thoughts as to whether people like you or not come into your mind, do not even look at them, for they will always like you as much as God wills."[20]

The relationships Francis de Sales built as a friend and counselor are numerous and laudable. They include a king, governors and princes, cardinals and popes, laity and religious. None, perhaps, is more notable than his friendship with Jane Frances de Chantal. At the time they met, this future saint had a very complex story and that story was undoubtedly the work of God from then on. She was the daughter of a powerful man, an unexpected widow, a mother of four, and highly convicted of God's voice calling her to religious life. Francis sought her out and made sure she was kept close with counsel, prayer, and discernment. Their saintly relationship is expressed in the beautiful letters they exchanged, which turned into some of Francis's most celebrated works. He always approached her needs with the utmost sincerity and gentleness, even when he needed to use stronger words to urge her direction.

Another famous friendship he enjoyed as counselor was with one Madame de Charmoisy, who met Francis in 1603. They exchanged many letters and had many private meetings. As a funny twist, her memory was not terribly good and he often had to repeat himself to her. Finally, he decided he needed to draft a longer letter to her as a sort of rule for her desired way of life, focused on personal devotion and holiness. These letters and others were bundled into what became one of Catholicism's most beloved devotions, *Introduction to the Devout Life*. This is the way, in fact, that most of his writings came to be published. He even remarked at the time, "I have written a book without knowing it." There was only one book he purposely wrote for publication—*Treatise on the Love of God*—and it took four years to complete because he was constantly writing letters.

These two relationships uncover an important trait of Francis's, which all aspiring apologists and counselors must adopt: *always speak and write as if you will be published*. If the sum of all our emails and social media comments were published one day, what would it say about us? Would it be memorable, moving, full of love and gentleness, or would it be literary junk food, gossip, and defiance? Francis de Sales never intended to be a writer but he always tried his best to give uplifting guidance to everyone who asked. He famously said, "Ask for nothing, refuse nothing." He never refused to give his best answer to those who rejected or misunderstood Scripture and Tradition, and always loved those who sought a deeper relationship with our Lord and better discernment for their vocation. To imitate him is simply to ask, who needs our help?

Conclusion

The synergistic value of being a good communicator and friend is pivotal to our success in bringing people "home" to the Catholic Church. After all, at home, people think alike and take care of one another. What we gather from the life of this Counter-Reformer, Francis de Sales, is a model of the harmony that should exist between the works of apologetics and evangelization: *relationship-building*.

As apologists we must be good communicators but we don't have to be master lecturers. Remember that Francis was scolded by his own father for using too-simple words. But who converted tens of thousands? Francis. The technique is undeniable. Francis advises us, "Use simple, homely words, likewise the transitions between ideas should be simply and readily grasped by all."[21]

His life should also inspire us to see no limitations no matter our circumstance. Francis was the bishop of Geneva, but he was never to sit in the episcopal chair of his own city. Because Geneva was overrun with Calvinists, he was relegated to administer his see from the nearby town of Annecy. But this did not stop him, and on many nights he would ride his horse door to door, street to street, dropping off tracts, encouraging the faithful, and reinstating parishes.

He executed this mission of peril with great bravery. Once, he was forced to pass through the main gate to the city where he would surely be recognized. Upon reaching the gate and receiving the standard interrogation of who he was and with what company he replied, "The diocese."

"The diocese?!" the guard said, puzzled. "Never heard of that place. Pass." And so Francis did.

Miracle or mistake, Francis de Sales answered his vocation with concern only for the souls of those he served. If we hope to reform the culture of our age, we must be like Francis: we must be powerful communicators of simple truths, and friends with good counsel.

Reading more about the life and works of Francis de Sales is worthwhile, and there are positively numerous books and essays that will keep even the most avid reader active. There's many biographies to choose from, and two excellent choices are Louise Stacpoole-Kenny's *St. Francis de Sales: A Biography of The Gentle Saint*, and an enduring classic from the man who personally knew the Doctor of the Church, *The Spirit of St. Francis de Sales* by Jean-Pierre Camus. For budding apologists, an insightful must read is Patrick Madrid's *On a Mission*, which tells us how to have the heart of an apostle, drawing from the life of our saint. The devotee has several to choose from Francis's own quill: *Introduction to the Devout Life, Treatise on the Love of God*, and any collection of his individual epistles to his flock and Jane Frances de Chantal.

Prayer for Writers

May the Lord guide me and all those who write. Through your prayers, St. Francis de Sales, I ask for your intercession as I attempt to bring the written word to the world. Let us pray that God takes me in the palm of his hand and inspires my creativity and inspires my success. St. Francis de Sales, you understand the dedication required. Pray for God to inspire and allow ideas to flow. In his name, let my words reflect my faith for others to read. Amen.

Offering One's Self to God

Lord, I am yours, and I must belong to no one but you. My soul is yours, and must live only by you. My will is yours, and must love only for you. I must love you as my first cause, since I am from you. I must love you as my end and rest, since I am for you. I must love you more than my own being, since my being subsists by you. I must love you more than myself, since I am all yours and all in you. Amen.

Chapter 2

St. Ignatius of Loyola
Reformer of Education and Spirituality

October 23, 1491–July 31, 1566
Feast Day: July 31

"To conquer himself is the greatest victory that man can gain."

Up to his twenty-sixth year the heart of Ignatius was enthralled by the vanities of the world. His special delight was in the military life, and he seemed led by a strong and empty desire of gaining for himself a great name. The citadel of Pampeluna was held in siege by the French. All the other soldiers were unanimous in wishing to surrender on condition of freedom to leave, since it was impossible to hold out any longer; but Ignatius so persuaded the commander, that, against the views of all the other nobles, he decided to hold the citadel against the enemy.

When the day of assault came, Ignatius made his confession to one of the nobles, his companion in arms. The soldier also made his to Ignatius. After the walls were destroyed, Ignatius stood fighting bravely until a cannon ball of the enemy broke one of his legs and seriously injured the other.

His recovery was very slow, and doctors and surgeons were summoned from all parts for a consultation.

They decided that the leg should be broken again, that the bones, which had knit badly, might be properly reset.[22]

Dictating his autobiography in the third person decades later, Ignatius must have looked back on this event with a completely different sentiment than he had when he was confined to an infirmary bed. He was in love with the world then, and was consumed with the idea of becoming famous. Ignatius was, like his leg bones, in need of a re-breaking. He realized in a physical and spiritual sense that he was broken, but would need to be broken again in order to completely heal to the right state: a state of life and purpose. His ambitions up to that point were purely material, seeking fame and glory for his kingdom, but God had purposed him for a different sort of fame and glory: the glory of uniting oneself to Christ, and building the heavenly kingdom.

Reformer of Self, First

Long before he instructed his followers to "go forth and set the world on fire," Ignatius was under his own fire of spiritual and physical combat. His leg was broken, as was his spirit. Legs take us to our destination, but Ignatius no longer knew where that destination was. His whole life he had perfected the profession of a soldier: exercise, training, wielding armor and weapons, imagining the enemy and visualizing victory.

Because he would never be a soldier again, he was convinced that his twenty-three years of life were useless, and that the rest of his life would be spend in the humiliation of defeat and the embarrassment of not being able to resurrect his former skills. On that same bed where he wished for death more than once, he would consider a different sort of death: a death to self. His physical exercises were about to become his famed *Spiritual Exercises*; he would put on the full armor of God (Eph. 6:11), wield his word as a sword (Eph. 6:17), and use his imagination to envision himself in victory for heaven.

In order to become this person God created him to be, he knew he must reform himself first, and in a saying often ascribed to him he instructs the same of us: "He who goes about to reform the world must begin with himself, or he loses his labor."[23]

His Counter-Reformation labors started with himself, and although he accomplished much and his life can teach us copious lessons of Christian charity and virtue, he dominates in two principle areas: education and spirituality.

Proper Education

> "The [Second Vatican Council] has considered with case how extremely important education is in the life of man and how its influence ever grows in the social progress of this age."—*Gravissimum Educationis*

Sacred art depicting Ignatius usually depicts him studying, reading, writing. It might surprise some to learn, then, that for the first half of his life Ignatius was not an educated man. Though his intellect was strong and his aptitude was high, our saint had less than a grammar-level education at the age of twenty-three, just a few years before he formed the Society of Jesus and founded colleges. He placed little emphasis on structured learning, perhaps because he was a soldier, yet still came to be one of the most respected educators of his time. What caused such a change? The answer is not so simple. To understand what he did, we need to understand his story.

After his leg was shattered in that cannonball blast, Ignatius's dreams of soldiery were gone. But as he said of himself
in his autobiography, "his special delight was in the military
life,"[24] so if he could not do these things he at least wanted
to fill his mind with the thoughts of others doing them. So
Ignatius requested books about valiant knights and heroes of
war, but there were none. Instead he was handed *The Life of
Christ* by Ludolph the Carthusian and a book about the lives
of the saints. At first he was reluctant to read either but soon
found himself engrossed in stories of the heroic virtue, if not
quite of the kind he had sought.

After he was healed he continued to study and grow in
devotion. He became a gifted street-teacher and built a small
following. This drew the attention of the clergy. Around this
time the Inquisition was rooting out any potential heresy or
corrupted preaching, and without a degree or formal training
Ignatius was looked at suspiciously. He was examined briefly
by the Inquisition but they found no error in his interview
and let him go—but did instruct him not to dress as if he
were clergy. He was later summoned again, and again they
found no error.

A last time he was examined by the Inquisition, whose
verdict resulted in an interesting action by Ignatius. Each time
prior, he had explained that he was not preaching or teaching novelties, but was simply conversing with small groups
about holy and divine things, occasionally introducing his
"exercises" still in development. This time, he was questioned
about his advice to others on faith and morals. In his own
autobiographical words:

> So clear and exact was his explanation that his examin-
> ers could not find the least flaw in his doctrine. He was
> equally correct in the answer to the friar who proposed

a difficulty in canon law. In every case he said that he did not know the decision of the professors.[25]

The tribunal's verdict was that Ignatius would be free to teach on matters of Christian doctrine, but not on sin or canon law. Not until, the tribunal said, he completed four years of study.

He accepted the decision, but found a loophole: since the inquisitors' verdict was limited to their local jurisdiction, he was able to preach a full message elsewhere. So he left Salamanca, studied for a while in Barcelona, and then began advanced studies in Paris.

Over the span of the next several years Ignatius traveled widely, sitting in classrooms for academic disciplines from liberal arts, philosophy, Latin, logic, and physics to, of course, theology. With fortitude, he received a degree from the University of Paris. He came to be a deep lover of education, and came to believe that its final purpose was to exalt and serve God. In order to serve God the best way possible, then, deep and rigorous schooling was necessary.

> Man is created to praise, reverence, and serve God our Lord, and by this means to save his soul. All other things on the face of the earth are created for man to help him fulfill the end for which he is created. From this it follows that man is to use these things to the extent that they will help him to attain this end. Likewise, he must rid himself of them in so far as they prevent him from attaining it.[26]

What to study, then? First, Ignatius believed in having a solid foundation for learning with good grammar. Though he was not completely illiterate, before his Paris studies he revisited the basics, studying with children. He writes about himself in his *Autobiography*:

At Paris, he lived with some Spaniards, and attended the lectures given at the College of Montaigu. As he had been advanced too rapidly to the higher studies, he returned to those of a lower grade, because he felt that in part he lacked the proper groundwork. He therefore studied in a class with children.[27]

It might sound trivial, but returning to the "basics" first can help go deeper into any given study or endeavor. Every semester of algebra or calculus opens with a "refresher," like athletes sometimes revisit the basics of technique and form. Any quality education in philosophy or theology, especially, begins with a study of basic principles and even vocabulary. A philosopher and theologian's lexicon and foundation must be precise, or else they risk error.

Ignatius also studied, and became a proponent of, the *humanities*. One of the principles of Ignatian spirituality is experience, and the study of literature, history, language, ethics, philosophy, and the like, gives us a foundation for experience.

But all these studies, says Ignatius, are undertaken in order to "enkindle . . . a desire for sacred theology and a love for it."[28] God is the highest subject of study. Theology is the queen of sciences because it helps us understand knowledge that we cannot discover by ourselves. Our study of theology culminates in the God who revealed himself, who wants to have a relationship with us. So, studying theology is not just an intellectual matter, but one of living our daily lives with purpose—a purpose that includes defending and sharing the truths of the Faith.

According to Ignatius, those who wish to make a study of theology must accomplish three things first. First, they must have a *real interest* in the study. Our saint was very blunt on the reason for this: "Without this interest and in-clination every class exercise will prove boring, and in the end there will be little progress."[29] After there is genuine interest, Ignatius insists upon a *proper foundation* in logic and philosophy, and also in languages.[30] Logic is indispensable in understanding fallacies, drawing proper conclusions, and helping us to judge the quality of arguments. Philosophy is crucial to studying theology because it improves critical thinking, ethical considerations, and developing interpretive faculties. For language, Ignatius recommends Latin, Greek, and Hebrew. Understanding even a little bit of these lan-guages greatly enriches our ability to go deeper into Sacred Scripture and ancient documents. Fortunately, we live in a time when widely available study aids make it easier than ever to acquire such knowledge.

Of course, Ignatius's emphasis on education was critical in training other Counter-Reformers to combat the heresies of the day. The success of such heresies, he said, "is largely due to the negligence of those who should have shown some interest, and the bad example and the ignorance of Catholics, especially the clergy, have made such ravages in the vineyard of the Lord."[31] In this context, he gives educational guidance that applies equally to those engaged in apologetics today:

> In the first place, sound theology, which is taught in the universities and must have its foundation in phi-losophy and which requires a long time to acquire, is adapted only to alert and agile minds; because the weaker ones, who lack a proper foundation, can be-come confused and collapse, it would be good to pre-pare a summary of theology dealing briefly with top-ics that are essential but not controversial. In matters controversial there could be more detail, but it should

be accommodated to the present needs of the people. It should solidly prove dogmas with appropriate arguments from Scripture, tradition, the councils, doctors, and refute the contrary teaching. It would not require too much time to teach such theology since it would not go very deeply into other matters. In this way, many theologians could be prepared in a short time, who could attend to preaching and teaching in various places. The abler students could be given advanced courses which include greater detail. Those who do not succeed in these advanced courses should be removed from them and placed in the shorter course of theology.[32]

Today there seems to be a vast amount of Catholic magazines, news sources, media resource outlets, blogs, vlogs, and discussion forums. All of these claim to be Catholic, but yet they often differ on important matters of faith and morals. There was no shortage of error and disagreement in Ignatius's day, either. This is exactly the reason the Inquisition was instituted, and the reason authorities investigated Ignatius's preaching. Our modern Catholic media are virtually ungoverned by clerical authorities, and so are left to the policing of knowledgeable, faithful Catholics who have the courage to speak out. This underscores the necessity for all of us to have a sound theological education, and to put that education to work in the service of the Faith. St. Ignatius notes:

The heretics write a good many pamphlets and booklets, by which they aim to remove all authority from the Catholics, and especially from the Society [of Jesus], and set up their false dogmas. It would seem imperative, therefore, that ours also write answers in pamphlet form, short and well written, so that they can be produced without delay and purchased by many. In this way the harm done by the pamphlets of the heretics can be set aright and sound teaching spread. These works should be modest, but stimulating; they should point out the evil that is abroad and uncover the deceits and evil purposes of the adversaries. Many of these pamphlets could then be gathered in a single volume. Care should be taken, however, that this be carried out by learned men well grounded in theology, who will adapt the content to the capacity of the multitude.[33]

With such measures we can bring true reform to the Church in times of need.

Whether it is our children, a classroom of college students, or an audience of media followers, each of us has the responsibility, within the context of our vocation, consideration of our abilities, and the grace that God gives us, to seek educational opportunities and to return the gift of knowledge to others. In doing so we must be careful to adhere to the principles of faith and remain mindful of good practices that put the well-being of others first. As an obedient soldier and unremitting student, Ignatius would have it no other way.

True Spirituality

All of us have heard someone say, "I'm spiritual but not religious." Yet this doesn't tell us much, because *spiritual* means different things to different people. Spirituality is difficult to describe precisely because of what St. Ignatius once observed in a letter to a Benedictine nun: "No one can explain another person's interior experiences as well as the person who is undergoing it."[34] And that's very true, but there *is* a means of defining spirituality: by analyzing its purpose, looking to God as our cause. We do this by asking *who, what,* and *why.*

Who are we? We are God's creations, and his children through his Son, Jesus Christ. *What* are we? We are human beings, fashioned in God's image and likeness, infused with a rational human soul. *Why* do we exist? To know, love, and serve God, and to share in his life. This is the "fundamental reason" for our dignity (CCC 356).

Each of the answers has one thing in common: God creating man. God created us in a specific way: he made us in his "image and likeness," signifying our capacity for knowledge, dignity, possession, and freely giving ourselves to others (CCC 357). We are both corporeal and spiritual. We are corporeal because we are material beings with a body; we are made from the "dust of the ground" (Gen. 2:7). We are spiritual because we have a soul (CCC 363) that animates our body with life, will, and intellect. The purpose of this soul being united with our bodies is to unite *us* as persons to God in the Body of Christ. What all of this means is that when we seek our soul and its purpose, we seek God. This is true spirituality. Because God is entirely spirit, and is the origin from and purpose for which everything else was made, seeking spirituality means seeking God.

How do we seek the spiritual life? It might not be a satisfying answer, but it's vitally important to recognize that *every single choice we make contributes to our spiritual life.* Every time we choose grudges or forgiveness, every time we pray or curse, every time we nap or work, every time we sin or love, we contribute to our spiritual life. Since our final spiritual state of perfection is the beatific vision, wherein our soul receives the capacity of immediately comprehending the sight of God (CCC 1028), everything we choose to do either enables or disables that end (CCC 1033).

Some things, of course, do more for our soul than others. As an ex-military man, Ignatius fell back on his training as an aid to understanding the spiritual life. As exercise and training aids a soldier in physical combat, he saw that there are religious exercises that aid the Christian in *spiritual* combat:

> This expression *Spiritual Exercise* embraces every method of examination of conscience, of mediation, of contemplation, of vocal and mental prayer, and of performing other spiritual actions . . . For just as strolling, walking, and running are bodily exercises, so spiritual exercises are methods of preparing and disposing the soul to rid itself of all inordinate attachments, and after accomplishing this, seeking and discovering the divine will regarding the disposition of one's life, thus insuring the salvation of his soul [is called Spiritual Exercise].[35]

If we want to be true reformers of our own lives and our works, we must study and imitate the spirituality of one of the first Counter-Reformers—indeed, the one who founded an order precisely for that purpose. Ignatius's life and writings focus on training in these key aspects of spiritual progress: holiness, prayer, service, mortifications, fasting, and discernment.

As we saw, the fundamental purpose of spirituality is seeking *holiness*, allowing God to seize our hearts. To be holy means allowing God to transform us, to convert us away from sin and toward him. The first part must happen before the second: we will never be able to cooperate with God's grace if we remain within the vise of sin. Christ said, "No one can serve two masters; for either he will hate the one and love the other, or he will be devoted to the one and despise the other" (Matt. 6:24). On this, St. Ignatius's words are straightforward: "Always avoid whatever things are harmful. If you avoid them, temptation will have no power over you. This is what you should be doing always, placing the Lord's praise ahead of everything else."[36]

It is no surprise, then, that discerning good and evil "spirits" is a chief purpose of his *Exercises*. His teaching on the subject is very helpful. In the opening words of Ignatius in his autobiography, he describes a simple mental exercise for avoiding sin. He describes himself as "enthralled by the vanities of the world" and, "led by a strong and empty desire of gaining for himself a great name." Now read his words during his conversion:

> When he thought of worldly things, it gave him great pleasure, but afterward he found himself dry and sad. But when he thought of journeying to Jerusalem, and of living only on herbs, and preaching austerities, he found pleasure not only while thinking of them, but also when he had ceased.[37]

The difference is stark and telling of the simplicity in this self-examination. The world gives us pleasure, but it doesn't last. The endeavors that give us pleasure long after we have contemplated or undertaken them are the ones we should pursue. Everything else is aversive to the spiritual life. Man can never sin unless he wills it, and too often, sin is a distortion of what our hearts really want. Sex is good, but only within the context of a proper union. Eating is healthy, but gluttony is wasteful and obsessive. When we are tempted to sin, one of the most helpful spiritual exercises we can take up is to consider the personal consequences of our sin, considering what our hearts truly want for happiness.

Avoiding sin is essential to spiritual development, the first door of many to the interior of the human person, to allowing

God to take over our hearts, of which the most important is *prayer*. Prayer is the basic act of the spiritual life, but many ignore it. Many pray only when they are in trouble or need something (or think they do). Even during Mass, when we recite prayers as a congregation, it's too easy just to say the words without attention. If the soul is the form of the body, then prayer is its food. Ignatius remarks:

> I must remind you to frequent the sacraments, to read spiritual books, and to pray with as much recollection as you possibly can. Every day set aside some time so that the soul will not be without its food and, thus, you will not be induced to complain like the one who said "My heart has withered because I have forgotten to eat my bread."[38]

Here Ignatius sets a perfect tone for prayer. Just as people who don't eat are physically malnourished, those who fail to pray are starving their souls. We should pray "every day" as Ignatius points out here, but what should we pray about? The answer is *everything!* St. Paul says, "Have no anxiety about anything, but in everything by prayer and supplication with thanksgiving let your requests be made known to God" (Phil. 4:6). Anything can cause us to have anxiety, and in that vein, we should put everything in our prayers: our hopes, fears, pleasures, habits, addictions, ambitions, successes and failures—*everything* should be committed to prayer. Even the very smallest things we can implicitly commit to prayer by simply saying, "Jesus, I trust you with everything. May your will be done, not mine."

Prayer takes many public and liturgical forms, but these are no substitute for private, focused prayer. Such prayer is the time to quiet the soul, to hash out what is concerning us or filling us with thankfulness, and then being silent and

attentive to what God puts on our heart. One common ex-
cuse for not praying is thinking that we have no effect on
God's foreknowledge or Providence. A person might say,
"I don't pray because I won't change God's mind and he
already knows what's going to happen, so I'm better off being content." Being content is great, but it's a mistake not to
recognize that God's Providence and foreknowledge work
together for our benefit. God's knowledge is outside of space
and time, which means he knows everything in a perfect
present, but obviously our knowledge is enormously limited
in comparison. Not only do we not know the future, but we
frequently forget what happened just last week. How then
should we be expected to apply all our experiences to life?
This is why we pray. God knows what will happen, but we
are given free will to judge and execute our actions, and
these either in assent to his purposes or in detraction of them.
When we pray, then, we are aligning ourselves to God's will.
St. Thomas Aquinas puts it this way:

> For we pray not that we may change the Divine dis-
> position, but that we may impetrate that which God
> has disposed to be fulfilled by our prayers in other
> words that by asking, men may deserve to receive
> what Almighty God from eternity has disposed to
> give.[39]

Many struggle with prayer out of general laziness and
distraction. Particularly, many fail to pray for others when
it's requested. There's two simple easy ways to combat this
immediately: immediately fold your hands and say a quick,
heartfelt prayer; or, if you're too busy, quickly cross yourself
with that intention on your heart. Some are very distracted
in prayer. Ignatius had an active (and sometimes distracting)
imagination, but used it to imagine what he was praying

about. If he wanted to seek a pilgrimage to Jerusalem, he imagined it and discerned its "spirit." He wrote down his requests and concerns and read them during prayer, and the moment he was distracted, he read them again.

Service is also another means of seeking true spirituality. As the superior general of the Society of Jesus, Ignatius had no hesitations in teaching that the spirituality we seek in daily prayer can be achieved through our daily activity. He told a group of priests and brothers studying in Coimbra, Portugal:

> The demands of your life of study do not permit you to devote much time to prayer, yet you can make up for this by desires, since the time you devote to your various exercises is a continuous prayer, seeing that you are engaged in them only for God's service.[40]

Our acts of service include not just what we do, but the spirit and care with which we do them. When we act with the purpose of serving God, we are making a fervent prayer. Likewise, when our efforts pursue perfection, we pursue God. In these ways, as our Counter-Reformer Ignatius agrees, we can ensure we complete the command of St. Paul to "pray constantly" (1 Thess. 5:17).

The practice of *mortification* is encouraged in the Bible. Paul made sure the Corinthians knew that he "pommeled" and "subdued" his flesh,[41] and Christ was clear about the effect of the body on the soul:

> And if your hand causes you to sin, cut it off; it is better for you to enter life maimed than with two hands to go to hell, to the unquenchable fire. And if your foot causes you to sin, cut it off; it is better for you to enter life lame than with two feet to be thrown into hell (Mark 9:43–45).[42]

But we must also approach the use of these penances with wisdom and direction. Ignatius endorsed the use of mortifications for taming the flesh,[43] instructing three things: they are essential to avoiding sin; they are not necessary for suppressing actions or desires that are licit (though moderately useful); and, bodily recreation can be of better service for some. On the first, he instructs a young scholastic whose body was becoming quite weak from the intensity of his mortifications. He offers:

> [W]hen the reason enlightened by God becomes aware of a movement of sensuality or of the sensitive part of nature against God's will, yielding to which would be a sin, you repress it through the fear and love of God. This is well done, even though some weakness should ensue or some bodily ill, since sin should not be committed for this or any other reason.[44]

As useful as bodily mortifications and penances are, though, Ignatius wisely instructs balance in the spiritual life. To a studying duke who secretly took vows to join the Jesuit order, Ignatius advised, "the time set aside for these exercises, both interior and exterior, should be reduced by half."[45] Ignatius is referring to penances of mortifications. What's the right mixture of prayer through action and prayer through spiritual penance?

> We ought to increase these [spiritual penances and mortifications] when our thoughts have their origin in ourselves or are suggested by our enemy, and lead us to fix our attention on objects that are distracting, frivolous, or forbidden, or when we wish to prevent our wills from taking any satisfaction in them or yielding any consent. I say, as a rule, that as these thoughts

multiply we ought to increase our exercises, both interior and exterior, so that we may overcome them, always keeping in mind the individual's character, the varying nature of the thoughts or temptations, and being careful to adapt the exercises to the capacity of the individual. However, when these thoughts weaken and die out, holy thoughts and inspirations will take their place.[46]

Writing again to Stefano Casanova, he clarifies a counter judgment: that some will have more benefit from physical training, that painful mortification "is neither good for all, nor should it be used at all times." Even more recreation, he says, can have greater benefit to some and give them a longer opportunity to serve God. This must have been the soldier in him coming out! In any case, penances and mortifications should arise and increase when our thoughts and motives are sinful or originate from sinful desires. The flesh and the mind are connected in the soul as the "form" of the human person, so when one is tamed, the other benefits. When penance and mortification have accomplished their purpose, we should decrease them as exercises and increase our contemplative exercises instead.

Ignatius also supplements the ascetic life with regular *fasting*. Again, this is a biblical practice. We see examples when the Lord's army was partially defeated (2 Sam. 1:12), when Daniel needed strength (Dan. 10:3), and when Esther did (Esther 4:16) and numerous other places in the Old Testament. The practice continues in the New Testament when Christians were sent off for missionary journeys (Acts 13:3-4), and Jesus is clear in the Sermon on the Mount when he says "*when* you fast" rather than "*if* you fast." Nearly every saint fasted in some fashion, but the normal fast consists of giving up food and beverages other than water. Ignatius fasted regularly. To do this, he kept his fasts limited to meager meals, almost never eating meats, and breaking his fasts on Sundays only if he was offered.

A basic fast most Catholics can undertake is to eat just one meal on one day every week. For some this will be a challenge, but others might require something more austere. As during Lent and Advent, though, we can also abstain by "giving up" something for a period of time. These can be anything associated with the flesh and pleasure, for all mortifications are for the benefit of taming the flesh in order to strengthen the soul.[47]

Ignatius has a real appreciation for balance in the spiritual life, respective to the professions, gifts, and circumstances of each person he directed. Where fasts and abstinences are concerned, he made sure to account for this.

> As to fasts and abstinences, I would advise you in our Lord to strengthen your stomach and your other physical powers, rather than to weaken them. My reason is that, in the first place, when a soul is so disposed to lose its own life rather than offend God's majesty by even the slightest deliberate sin and is, moreover, comparatively free from the temptations of the world, the flesh, and the devil . . . since both body and soul are gifts from your Creator and Lord, you should give him a good account of both. To do this you must not allow your body to grow weak; for if you do, the interior man will no longer be able to function properly. Therefore though I once highly praised fasting and abstinence, even from many ordinary foods, and for a certain period was pleased with this program, I cannot now praise it when I see that the stomach, because of

these fasts and abstinences, cannot function naturally or digest any of the ordinary meats or other items of diet which contribute to the proper maintenance of the body.[48]

The ascetical life of Ignatius is reflective of the grace that was given to him: his fasts were extreme and should not be imitated without the direction and consent of a spiritual director, but this does not mean that we can ignore the requirement to fast. We must supplicate our prayer with fasting without exception, but we also must be careful not to.

True spirituality involves *discernment* for our will, which is cooperative with God's. It's easy to want God just to give us the information we need to carry out his will. And it would be easy for God to do that. As much as we try to convince ourselves that receiving these signs and revelations would enable us to masterfully achieve his will for us, they might actually help us very little. Those watching Jesus' crucifixion demanded a sign, as did his accusers, and even Herod. A sign might have greatly scared them into behaving differently, but the spiritual life goes much deeper than behavior modifications.

Ignatius's *Spiritual Exercises* are mainly concerned with discernment, or choice. Since all spirituality is a seeking of God, we are constantly provided choices that either seek God or turn away from him. (Anyone wishing to make a retreat or undertaking the exercises will be best off consulting a priest or layman who is well acquainted with the technique.) Ignatius provides us with an "if all else fails" way of knowing what God wants us to do:

> Earthly concerns have no place in your thoughts or affections, you will be preserved from distraction and dissipation, so that you will be able to direct your

thoughts and affections and employ them in attaining the end for which God created you: that is, his own honor and glory, your own salvation, and the help of your neighbor. It is true that all orders in the Church are directed to this end.[49]

And:

If you are very busy, you should make a choice and employ yourself in the more important occupations where there is greater service of God, greater spiritual advantage for the neighbor, and the more general or perfect good. Keeping a little time to put order in yourself and your activities will be of considerable help to you in this respect.[50]

Any end in our discernment will advance the commandment to serve God by serving others. In this, St. Ignatius assures us, the assistance of the saints is invaluable: "The good disposition and devotion of your patrons will be a great help to you in setting to order what should be better arranged." As he was in recovery from his wounds, he developed a great admiration for the saints and desired to imitate them. His actions say it all: when we are unaware of what to do or how to follow God, we can never fail by imitating the saints.

Conclusion

There are many ways to become a saint, and the first starts with becoming familiar with those who are already saints. This is exactly what St. Ignatius did, even though he was apprehensive in the beginning, wanting something more that his idea of God, and hopeful for a glorious and noble death. In a way, he got what he wanted, and much more. That road led to him becoming one of the most educated people of all time with studies in numerous disciplines. His knowledge was bountiful, and he encouraged everyone he discipled to pursue an education that resulted in an appreciation of the human person, service to others, and knowledge of divine things. No matter the level of study, we should pursue the same with diligence and prayer.

Maintaining our bodily health is very important, but our spiritual health is vastly more important. The world will always offer a replacement of God or a substitute for spiritual nourishment, but they are all tepid and empty, which is why spiritual fads are constantly traded in and out, generation after generation. Ignatius offers crucial guidelines for our spiritual health, and if we follow them closely we'll be sure to resist temptations, sanctify our souls, and become closer to God. True spirituality is robust, flavorful, and always ripe. It is also difficult. True spirituality consists of seeking holiness, and devotion to God by prayer, service to our neighbor, penance, fasting, and discernment. There is no replacement for any of these.

An old saying, sometimes attributed to Ignatius, counsels, "Act as if everything depended on you; trust as if everything depended on God." Reading the life of this saint will leave no minds doubting that he fully lived up to this judiciousness. Here is a saint who, even before he had a personal conversion, harvested good habits in discipline, integrity, and passion for service to others. Anything he did in his life was to the utmost pursuit of excellence. We should consider the same in anything we set out to accomplish.

Further devotion to St. Ignatius of Loyola should start with a quiet and thoughtful reading of his *Autobiography*. A good reason his conversion story is so popular is because, unlike the majority of other saints, it is in his own words. Through his recollection, we get a sense of what he considered important, worthwhile, and what else he considered vain. He considers his ego prior to the humbling defeat and eventual conversion, and still, his inability to quit anything he put his mind to. It is an epic read, recommended to all. Of course, there is his *Spiritual Exercises*, a book which is better read with the company of someone who is practiced in this specific contemplative art. Lastly, there are some versions of his selected writings that are superior in their simple and straightforward direction, covering numerous topics on spirituality, education, and living a holy life.

Anima Christi

The *Anima Christi* ("Soul of Christ") is richly associated with St. Ignatius of Loyola and Ignatian spirituality as it appears in the beginning of his *Spiritual Exercises*, even though he was not the original author. Still, he prayed it often, and one thoughtful reading of this modest prayer will aid us in gaining strength, consolation, and discernment.

> Soul of Christ, sanctify me.
> Body of Christ, save me.
> Blood of Christ, inebriate me.
> Water from the side of Christ, wash me.
> Passion of Christ, strengthen me.
> O good Jesus, hear me.

Within your wounds conceal me.
Do not permit me to be parted from you.
From the evil foe protect me.
At the hour of my death call me.
And bid me come to you,
to praise you with all your saints
for ever and ever.
Amen.

Chapter 3

St. Teresa of Ávila
The Mystical Reformer

March 28, 1515–October 4, 1582
Feast Day: October 15

"Truth suffers, but never dies."

Growing up in a rapidly changing Spain that included re-shaping her hometown, Ávila, the story of this Doctor of the Church is both improbable and unforgettable. From her earliest memories she desired to become a hermit, perhaps even a martyr. A brother who was close to her in age was a bosom friend who shared her desire to live a virtuous life-style by imitating the saints they heard and read about. They made plans to travel to the land of the Moors and beg them, out of a love for God, to have their heads cut off.

But the real outcome of St. Teresa's life would be a different kind of martyrdom. She would suffer early years without a mother, and struggle with attachment to her beauty and charm. Later in life, she would cover much of her face in the habit of a Carmelite nun, and prosper in a beauty defined by her friendship with God.

The woman who opened up the heavens with her understanding of prayer and communion with God, was also one of the chief Counter-Reformers. Reform did not come easy for this meek and docile cloistered nun, though. Her friends were beaten and thrown into jail, and she herself was the target of numerous threats from her enemies. She was wary to trust the authorities over her, but with the wisdom that came with her devotion and experience, she was able to lead a band of reformers and make allies in places she least expected.

A Model for Reform

The work of any true reformer is rooted in ideas and efforts that contribute to improvement rather than novelty. But Teresa's reform also created something new: the Discalced Carmelites. Her intention was not rooted in division, but when she realized that change was necessary in order to preserve the historical method of the Carmelite life, she was compelled to do something. Though she has a tremendous amount of opposition, she did gain the respect and backing of many influential leaders. So she wasn't lone-wolfing it—she would never advise such a mistake.

Perhaps Teresa's reform was less something new than a return to something old: the primitive Rule of Carmel, which had been gradually relaxed many years earlier to before remotely similar to that of the original order, contributing to a malaise of spiritual decline and corruption. She founded a set of new monasteries, enacted many positive changes—even though she would not live to see them all—and gifted the Church with a titanic advancement on the theology and practice of prayer. Her efforts were never aimed at making a name for herself, but they would eventually put her among the most important figures in the Counter-Reformation—and make her a great model for our own spiritual reform.

Graceful Opposition

Obedience comes natural to souls. Our nature is pleased by structure and authority. In life, we learn to value the natural structure of families, education, and work. We also learn, as we continue to understand structure, the importance the dynamics between leadership, management, and subsidiary. Some people learn structure and submission at an early age; they know who is in charge and how much power comes with that. Others may develop a certain resistance to rule and authority, perhaps from experiencing unjust authority (or little to no authority) during childhood.

There are natural strengths and weaknesses for those who are comfortable with authority and those who chafe against it. For the naturally obedient, there is the ability to follow instructions with great skill, but their creative talents might not develop as best they can. They know what to do and how to do it, but they might not blossom as an individual. Conversely, those who balance obedience with their independence can come up with new ideas, challenges to the status quo, and can offer solutions to problems and correction to abuses. Take note that these people ideally *balance* obedience and their ideas—they are not outright revolutionaries. Those who venture too far into individualism flirt with relativism, which is a disease to society and to true reform.

Teresa struggled to be obedient to people she either didn't trust or didn't have a working relationship with, but she understood the duty of obedience—to the Church she wanted to reform and to her superiors in religious life. She tells of her new confessor, Fr. Jerome Gratian, and how little she loved him at first, but how her desire for goodness enabled her willingness to trust and confide in the friar.

> I recalled that although I had made a vow of obedience, it wasn't of a kind I could obey with perfection . . . [I]f you don't get along with one superior, there is finally a change, and another one comes along; and that this promise would mean remaining without any freedom either interiorly or exteriorly throughout life.[51]

Perhaps Teresa, in her way, was being a little dramatic about the uncertainties of her future freedoms, but her honesty about her fear is telling of a conundrum she was facing: fulfill her vow of obedience and risk being flustered her whole life, or break her vow and live with the guilt. She tells us, furthermore, that she came to the critical realization that she did not make a promise to mere men, but to God.

> And at this point I knelt down and promised that for the rest of my life I would do everything Master Gratian might tell me, as long as there was nothing in opposition to God or my superiors to whom I was obliged.[52]

Her initial resistance was eventually overcome by her greater desire to be true to her perpetual vows to obey the Church and God, and it paid off. The history of the reforms of the Carmelite Order tell us that Fr. Gratian became a champion of our saint's efforts and aided her greatly in gaining political support in the province for the founding of her new monasteries under the Teresian reforms. She later remarked of this formation process, "And although I feared I might be restricted, I was left with greater freedom." Their mutual respect for each other enabled a mutually fruitful partnership. Fr. Gratian would later remark, "She taught me everything she knew, giving me so many doctrines, rules, and counsels that I could have written a large book about what she taught me."[53]

Teresa's example shows us that when we let go of every-thing and let our will align with God's will, we grow in a freedom that allows us to perform the works, corporal and spiritual, that we were created for. Many times, graceful oppo-sition means giving obedience a chance when we don't want to.

Having a solid foundation in obedience is strictly neces-sary to true reform, in the Church as well as in our souls; just as important as the reason for reform. We all grow dis-satisfied with one thing or another (or many things!). We might become unhappy with our jobs, but does that mean we should reform the company or does it mean we should switch careers? We might become displeased with our parish, but does that mean we should work to better the place or leave it entirely? When we think of reform, we also should be mindful that our first course of action is to look at our-selves. Is our disappointment merely a matter of poor attitude? Brashness? Factual errors? Grudges? If so, we need to focus on reforming ourselves first.

Teresa's reform originated in her ideas of prayer and the monastic life, and had much to do with the milieu present in late-medieval Spain. She was deeply influenced by many of her peers and those in authority over her, but none more than Cardinal Cisneros and John of Ávila, a lesser-known Doctor of the Church who prepared a path for her reforms all over Spain.

We've seen numerous examples of how reform can work in the history of the Catholic Church. Typically it involves a regimen or clarification, as opposed to a total abandonment or introduction of novelties. It could be the need to define a dogma, rather than abandoning and destroying icons. The reform might be a revision to the Mass—not an expunging of the Mass in total. Reform could require the administration of special disciplines like the suppression of the *Humiliati* by

St. Charles Borromeo and Pope Pius V, rather than inspiring and enabling a schism.[54]

Her monastery had suffered a spiritual malaise, specifically, a lack of desire to adhere to the primitive rules of the Carmelite order, and in her time, had even relaxed the cloister—purposed to promote, protect, and develop the practice of prayer and contemplation—to the point where the monastery lost its identity. She wanted to do something about it.

A valuable lesson we can learn from her reforms is the dynamic between self-doubt and self-satisfaction. Teresa struggled for years wondering if her ideas for reform and her dissatisfaction with her vocational life were new residents in her soul or vagabond feelings. Was her desire for reform aimed at helping the Church, or Teresa?

First she looked at herself to see if and where *she* needed reform. In reading her works, we become quickly aware of her criticisms of herself and her self-acknowledgment of personal shortcomings. The opening to her autobiography reads: "To have had virtuous and God-fearing parents . . . would have been enough . . . if I had not been so wicked."[55] She does the same in the introduction to her memoirs on the founding of her reformed order: "I confess, first of all, my imperfect obedience at the outset of this writing."[56] So, the fact that she pressed on (after a long discernment process) is not an indication of her lack of humility. Therefore, our first and foremost lesson in graceful reform is to look at ourselves: it is folly to go around thinking that our displeasure means the world needs to change to suit us. Rather, we first must look honestly at ourselves for change because the world and the Church owe us nothing—we owe the world love as Samaritan pilgrims and the Church service as citizens of heaven.

Then we must flee from the temptation to dismiss any amount of opposition as evil. Many times, pushback is the basic and most appropriate style for reform, even simple reforms in our daily life. If we never second guessed ourselves or others, there is no telling how things could get out of control. This dynamic is true in the workplace, at home, and in the Church. Seeking others for advice—and criticism—and letting God provide us with what is necessary for his work, is critical to reform success.

Moreover, whether reform is interior or external, it will require interior growth and conversion. Teresa would only be ready for religious reform when she was fully matured as a religious woman. And so she built her reforms on a quiet and careful confidence. She would eventually say,

> [A]fter the foundations were begun, the fears I previously had in thinking I was deceived left me. I grew certain the work was God's, and so I threw myself into difficult tasks, although always with advice and under obedience. As a result I understand that since our Lord desired to revive the original spirit of this order, and in his mercy he took me as a means, his Majesty had to provide me with what I was lacking, which was everything, in order to get results and better manifest his greatness.[57]

After years of discerning this desire, she began to check her ideas with others in the order and, perhaps more importantly, those authorities outside the order. Her work included collaboration with Dominicans, Jesuits, secular governors, and King Philip II of Spain. Through this political generosity and community-based perspicacity, she generated support and confirmed her own ideas without being a loose cannon.

Not all the opposition Teresa faced was just or constructive, which we see, for example, in the case of the kidnapping and incarceration of her co-reformer, St. John of the Cross. A virtue she used to her benefit in this time was *fortitude*. She relays this instruction to us: "I would never counsel anyone . . . to fail out of fear to put a good inspiration to practice when it repeatedly arises."[58]

Reform is a serious business. Teresa of Ávila teaches us that to treat it with the seriousness it deserves means, first, to be true to the obedience of our faith; second, be sure we have a proper need of and motive for reform; and third, ensure that others with proper authority understand and support the ideas (we think that) God puts on our heart. Although Teresa did not live to see the formation of the Discalced Carmelites— neither did St. John of the Cross—she laid a firm foundation by being an unfaltering example of good judgment and obedience. She knew she couldn't do everything, and had to leave some of the work to her commitment to obedience. In that vein, she lets us in on her secret: "This is true humility: to know what you can do, and what I can do."[59]

Prayer: The Key to the Castle

With her drive and perseverance to reform the Carmelite Order, Teresa also provided the Church with some of the most monumental and reliable works devoted to the subject of *prayer*. It is the constant theme in her writing throughout her life—whether as a young woman wanting to die for the Faith, or in her middle years when she was attached to worldly things, she refers to the condition of her prayer life. Teresa's vivid counsel in the opening paragraphs of her famous work *The Interior Castle* prompt us, "A short time ago I was told by a very learned man that souls without prayer are like people whose bodies or limbs are paralyzed: they possess feet and hands but they cannot control them."[60]

In *The Interior Castle* she allegorically connects the prayer life of a Christian with the structure of and life inside a castle.

Let us now imagine a castle, as I have said contains many mansions, some above, others below, others at each side; and in the center and midst of them all is the chiefest mansion where the most secret things happen between God and the soul.[61]

"You must think over this comparison very carefully," she warns. *Castle* extricates seven mansions; we'll look at the first three.

These mansions are states of the prayer life and the well-being of the soul, each measuring a closeness to God. Teresa points out that there are "many ways of being in a place." For example, we might be in the outer courts of a castle and never consider what it's like to be inside the throne room, or never work to take shelter from the harmful elements of the outside world. We might even attend the banquet dinner but never open our eyes and know we are there or that we are feasting with the king! Likewise, we can go to Mass every Sunday, but it does not necessarily mean that we are paying attention, participating, and contemplating the sacrifice present at the altar. We might never acknowledge that Christ is present in the Eucharist, or that we are surrounded by a cloud of witnesses. Of course, we desperately want to quit roaming the grounds of the castle and enter inside where the fire of God's love warms our hearts.

This is the first mansion of the lowest and outermost part of the castle. Souls here might be in a state of grace, but they suffer from frequent sin. Teresa says they sometimes let in reptiles as they enter in and out, which is a way of saying they are still largely attached to the things of the world—things that creep close to the earth—which is why they remain so close to the door.

We all want to be in the castle, but the only way in is "prayer and meditation." We cannot even hope to enter into closeness with God without them. It's then important to clarify which sort of prayer Teresa is pointing out. She does that for us:

> I do not say mental prayer rather than vocal, for, if it is prayer at all, it must be accompanied by meditation. If a person does not think whom he is addressing, and what he is asking for, and who it is that is asking and of whom he is asking it, I do not consider that he is praying at all even though he may be constantly moving his lips.[62]

Mental prayer is distinguished from vocal prayer, but even vocal prayer must have an element of meditation. Does this mean the rosary is a poor way to pray since we are "constantly moving our lips?" No. That's not what Teresa is alluding to here. She is warning against any prayer, even repetitive and rehearsed ones, that we have no conscious involvement with: we must remain mindful, purposeful, and anticipative in our prayer. To give an example, have you ever read a book and reached the end of the paragraph or page only to realize you were thinking of something else even though it was somewhat familiar to you upon a more attentive second reading? That's what thoughtless prayer is like. Teresa continues to clarify for us:

> True, it is sometimes possible to pray without paying heed to these things, but that is only because they have been thought about previously; if a man is in the habit of speaking to God's Majesty as he would speak to his slave, and never wonders if he is expressing himself properly, but merely utters the words that come to

his lips because he has learned them by heart through constant repetition, I do not call that prayer at all—and God grant no Christian may ever speak to him so![63]

Her wisdom is refreshingly clear: pray with mindful, purposeful, and anticipatory disposition, and you'll enter this first mansion. Keep it up, and you'll enter the next as well.

The next mansion is for those who have "already begun to practice prayer and who realize the importance of not remaining in the first mansions," but these souls "often are not yet resolute enough to leave those mansions, and will not avoid the occasions of sin, which is a very perilous condition."[64] What's unique about this condition of the soul is that they hear the voice of God calling them, distinguished from the noise of the outside world beyond the castle walls. Here, the souls don't just recognize the voice of the Lord, but enjoy an enhanced understanding of his mercy as well. This is not usually the still and small voice, but rather a voice these occupants hear through sermons, conversations with holy people, or through reading good books.

If the key to getting into the castle is prayer, and must become more practiced and frequent to enter this second mansion, then the next mansion is accessed by discerning the perfect will of God.

> All the beginner has to do—and you must not forget this, for it is very important—is to labor and be resolute and prepare himself with all possible diligence to bring his will into conformity with the will of God. This comprises the very greatest perfection which can be attained on the spiritual road.[65]

The "will of God" can seem intimidating. And rightfully so, because God's will is perfect and is not for us to be entertained by, to fool around with, or to take lightly. Pursuing the will of God and avoiding sin are intimately connected because sin clouds judgment and is so diametrically opposed to God that it paralyzes our faculties to the point where the lights are turned off spiritually. Hearkening in her statement on the disabling power of sin in the opening of *The Interior Castle,* she offers in another essay, "I was also shown how a soul in sin is without any power, but is like a person completely bound, tied, and blindfolded; for although wanting to see, such a person cannot, and cannot walk or hear, and remains in great darkness."[66]

To discern God's will with the highest chance of success, a soul should avoid sin to the highest degree possible. This "highest degree possible" includes ridding ourselves of the *opportunities* to sin: keeping our thoughts away from sinful things (and our previous sins), protecting ourselves from occasions and instruments of temptation, and so on. When we do sin, even venially, frequent reception of the sacrament of reconciliation enables our souls to be receptive to the graces and voice of God. This is how we stay in the second mansion, and render ourselves capable of venturing into the third mansion of the interior life, closer to God.

The death of Teresa's mother when Teresa was only fourteen filled her with grief, but she used this loss to further devote herself to a new mother: the Blessed Virgin Mary. For years, she clung to the Blessed Virgin and Jesus as close companions when she had little other comfort. This lasted until her early adult life when she became attached to the world and to possessions, to pleasing people and being socially and physically attractive. She practiced prayer, but without the completeness of meditation and detachment from the world. She was in the second mansion and remained there for several years even after she entered the convent. Multiple times she went from a high state of the interior life to an outer room in the castle. Perhaps she is further qualified to teach of such hazards in the spiritual life and the detail of these mansions because they were so familiar to her.

When she was finally able to progress into a more permanent state of devotion to the Lord, she better understood the third mansion, the exemplary mansion of which the Christian should aim. The third mansion is the place in which, despite his imperfections, a Christian is wholly committed to pleasing the Lord. In this mansion our contrition remains perfect, and our desire to love God is constant. Teresa explains:

> They are most desirous not to offend his Majesty; they avoid even committing venial sins; they love doing penance; they spend hours in recollection; they use their time well; they practice works of charity toward their neighbors; and they are very careful in their speech and dress and in the government of their household if they have one.[67]

Here in the third mansion we are further perfected because we are *performing good works*, rather than merely abstaining from bad habits. Teresa encourages us a bit further: "This is certainly a desirable state and there is no reason why they should be denied entrance to the very last of the mansions."

There are four additional mansions in the interior castle, each of which is considered mystical or consisting of contemplative prayer. In the fourth mansion, the person acquires less on his own effort, while God begins to provide more through his grace. The fifth mansion is a state where God has taken over—and it might last a short time—and provides a period of union in which the soul is preparing to receive a gift from God. Teresa refers to this mansion as a state of betrothal; indicating our imminent union with God. The sixth and penultimate mansion continues from there to a deeper intimacy between lover and beloved, where the soul gains increasing favors and—like many actual betrothals— certain afflictions to further test the strength of this impending marriage. Some afflictions are interior, some are exterior: dryness, persecution, sickness, and grief. The soul wants to be free of these, but only by way of the seventh mansion—union with our heavenly spouse; bliss, perfect peace where the only higher conceivable state is the beatific vision.

Now that the first three mansions of the interior castle are opened, we are ready to explore the practical suggestions that Teresa provides us as we aspire to enter and inhabit them. The principal message she wants every soul to know is that prayer is for everybody: beginners and advanced. Beginners need prayer to become closer to God and to conform to his will, while the advanced need prayer in order to sustain their spiritual gifts and for the imminent times of dryness and burnout. She says in her autobiography, "As for the man who has not begun to pray, I beg him for the love of our Lord not to forgo this great blessing. Here there is no place for fear, only for desire."[68]

She mentions fear because those in the first mansions are so prone to its temptations and ruinous power over the soul. Beginners worry that God will not hear their prayer, that they are not worthy, that they should not pray because they will only continue to sin; they even worry that there might not be a God, and so on. Each time we desire prayer, even a little, we should have peace that that desire only comes from the prompting of the Holy Spirit. Anything contrary, even a little, should motivate us to pray because it is certainly the evil one tempting us away from communion with God. To those with fear Teresa offers:

I can say what I know by experience—namely, that no one who has begun this practice, however many sins he may commit, should never forsake it. For it is the means by which we may amend our lives again, and without it, amendment will be very much harder . . . If we repent and truly determine not to offend him, he will resume his former friendship with us and grant us the favors which he granted aforetime, and sometimes many more, if our repentance merits it.[69]

If you're a beginner, have no fear! Be secure in trusting that there is *nothing* to fear: not even fear itself. She explains: "I don't understand what they fear who fear to begin the practice of mental prayer. I don't know what they are afraid of. The devil is doing his task well of making the truth seem evil."[70]

Getting to a more secure place inside the castle comes with time, devotion, and perseverance. Eventually, you'll desire prayer more, you'll overcome your sins, and you'll learn to recognize when Satan and his demons are talking you out of prayer and when God and his angels are encouraging you toward it. Remember, many Christians are beginners, but they're still inside the castle. Aim high, glorify God with your gratitude, and don't envy the spirituality of others.

From time to time, however, they shake their minds free of [their preoccupations] and it is a great thing that they should know themselves well enough to realize that they are not going the right way to reach the castle door . . . Still, they have done a good deal by entering at all.[71]

If you're in the second mansion you likely realize that being a Christian requires a lot of work, and good prayer requires good routine. You've got the routine down, but it's poor quality—how to improve it? First, Teresa says, get rid of your *distractions*. She had this same issue for nearly eighteen years! "And very often, for some years, I was more anxious that the hour I had determined to spend in prayer be over than I was to remain there, and more anxious to listen for the striking of the clock than to attend to other good things."[72]

First, get rid of the actual distractions: the ticking clock, the thump of loud music, nearby candy, the harsh lights—whatever it is, get rid of it. For mental distractions, consider using vocal prayer like an Our Father, a Hail Mary, or a verse of Scripture. Vocal prayer will help you set the mood and mindset for what's next: mental prayer. (For more on distractions in prayer, check up on further reading in the opening chapters of St. Teresa's autobiography.)

Once you're past the throes of trying to pray in the midst of distractions, begin to once again distinguish mental prayer from vocal prayer. Teresa explains mental prayer as "nothing else than an intimate sharing between friends; it means taking time frequently to be alone with him who we know loves us. In order that love be true and the friendship endure, the will of the friends must be in accord."[73] This type of prayer is a "language of love," which is when prayer becomes less of a duty and obligation—though it still is—and more natural, as conversation between spouses.

This type of prayer, unfortunately, is a bit deeper than our space allows, and any further discovery of it should occur with a spiritual director or a counselor. Here, we must realize that in the second mansion there begins a graduation from rehearsed or read "vocal prayer," to a more discursive prayer of loving ambition for heaven and communion with God.

If you can make prayer a consistent part of your life, and seek vocal and mental prayer that is free of distractions, the door to the third mansion of the castle is simple to enter through. Whatever you do, don't give up.

And you must believe that if you give up prayer, you are, in my opinion, courting danger.[74]

When you reach the third mansion, Teresa points to three colossal challenges that many souls will face: spiritual pride, dryness, and sin.

Spiritual pride could be a last-resort tool of the devil, who knows that many people are prone to looking down on others when they have reached an apex. This arrogance does not come immediately, but gradually over the course of time. However humble we may have been, we increasingly become disappointed with the sloths around us, or with changes in our communities and parish, creating bitterness and resentment. Anything bad that happens, we blame others. In whichever way the arrogance forms and takes appearance, it's a menace to the soul and should be avoided at all costs. Here's how Teresa puts it:

I have known a few souls who have entered [the third mansion]—I think I might even say a great many—and who, as far as we can see, have for many years lived an upright and carefully ordered life, both in soul and in body; and then, after all these years, when it has seemed as if they have gained the mastery over the world, or at least must be completely detached from it, his majesty has sent them tests which have been by no means exacting and they have become so restless and depressed in spirit that they have exasperated me, and have even made me thoroughly afraid of them.

It is no use offering them advice, for they have been practicing virtue for so long that they think they are capable of teaching others and have ample justification for feeling as they do.

Well, I cannot find, and have never found, any way of comforting such people, except to express great sorrow at their trouble, which, when I see them so miserable, I really do feel. It is useless to argue with them, for they brood over their woes and make up their minds that they are suffering for God's sake, and they never really understand that it is all due to their own imperfection. And in persons who have made so much progress this is a further mistake.[75]

As a permanent fixture in our spiritual life, it's best to avoid and hint of this type of elitism by a cultivating a constant sense of humility.

Teresa also warns of *dryness*, which is inevitable for all Christians but especially threatening to those who are so filled by spiritual pleasures that they depend on those pleasures to increase and sustain their spiritual fitness and works. This kind of temperament comes with high risk, for eventually there will come a period where we will gain little to no spiritual enjoyment from prayer, reading, devotions, Mass, and other spiritual exercises. If we base our desire to perform and take part in these activities out of sensual pleasure or gratification, when we encounter the dryness we will surely be sifted like chaff. Teresa explains in her autobiography:

> [W]hat will they do here who see that after many days there is nothing but dryness, distaste, vapidness, and very little desire to come to draw water? So little is the desire to do this that if they don't recall that doing so

serves and gives pleasure to the Lord of the garden, and if they aren't careful to preserve the merits acquired in this service . . . they will abandon everything.[76]

As a remedy, when we do things out of obligation we are far better off. If we also get enjoyment from spiritual things, great. But don't rely on that gratification.

Teresa of Ávila offers substantial teaching in prayer and her words should be considered by everyone wanting to journey into the mansions of spirituality, which are allegories for communion with God—our ultimate goal. Those who enjoy a life of holiness, purity, and closeness with God, Teresa maintains that "The path of self-knowledge must never be abandoned, nor is there on this journey a soul so much a giant that it has no need to return to the stage of an infant and a suckling."[77]

Conclusion

Her life didn't go how she thought it would, and that's true for nearly all of her years. From wanting martyrdom as a child and feeling alone as a teen, to eagerly pursuing popularity as a young adult, and still for the nearly two decades that she struggled to *really* desire the habit, she didn't know where she was headed. Even the Carmelite Order that she labored for years to improve would not see a final change until after she had died. It's smart to discover the perspective she provides: "Let nothing trouble you, nothing scare you. All is fleeting. God alone is unchanging. Patience everything obtains."[78] Be patient with the prayer you seek, be patient in discerning the changes you desire, and be patient in the work you do for the Lord. God will take care of everything else. Close to her death, after a life of petitioning popes and kings, she was able to say with unreserved poise: "At the end, Lord, I am a daughter of the Church."[79] Be the Church, reform to improve, not invent.

Whoever desires more knowledge of and closeness to this saint should be ready for the long haul! Her writings are crammed with knowledge, and her saintly perfections are difficult to achieve and require an extraordinary cooperation with God's grace. Nonetheless, any Christian can make strides if he reads and prays with sincerity. *The Interior Castle* is a masterpiece that commands the attention of all. Three volumes of her "collected works" are very worthwhile and, in addition to a translation of *Castle*, include her autobiography, her writings about the foundations, and dozens of other letters and poems she composed.

Prayer of St. Teresa of Ávila

Let nothing trouble you
Nothing scare you
All is fleeting
God alone is unchanging
Patience everything obtains
Who possesses God
Nothing wants
God alone suffices.[80]

Chapter 4

St. Robert Bellarmine
Our Model Apologist

October 4, 1542–September 17, 1621
Feast Day: September 17

"Freedom of belief is pernicious;
it is nothing but the freedom to be wrong."

In the cold waking hours of a late February day early in the seventeenth century, a council formed by Pope Paul V met in Rome to decide how the Church should deal with one brilliant yet egotistical scientist. The world had been turned upside down with his discoveries when he turned his "spy glass" to the heavens and saw images that no human in history had before. His discoveries were not just distant from earth; they were distant from the minds of all who heard the rushing news: the earth is not the center of the galaxy, multiple moons revolve around Jupiter (and other planets), and the earth orbits the sun.

Galileo's discovery took the world by storm, and Rome was eager to receive the bright scholar. After several private audiences where clergy and lay scholars were able to realize the finding with Galileo's own testimony, lectures, and aid, his popularity took shape. However, there was another group more cautious about the finding.

Half a century before, the Council of Trent had laid down specific rules for the treatment of new ideas. Chief among these was that no teaching or interpretation of Sacred Scripture may contradict the Church Fathers. The fourth session of the council reads:

> Furthermore, in order to restrain petulant spirits, it decrees, that no one, relying on his own skill, shall, in matters of faith, and of morals pertaining to the edification of Christian doctrine, wresting the Sacred Scripture to his own senses, dare to interpret the said Sacred Scripture contrary to that sense which holy mother Church, whose it is to judge of the true sense and interpretation of the holy Scriptures, hath held and doth hold; or even contrary to the unanimous consent of the fathers; even though suchlike interpretations were never [intended] to be at any time published. They who shall contravene shall be made known by their ordinaries, and be punished with the penalties by law established.[81]

Though Galileo's findings were completely factual and warranted the attention of rulers temporal and spiritual, his desire for success was such that he wanted the recognition overnight. But, however much the Church is dedicated to science, it is also careful, taking any and all time necessary to query, investigate, and confirm.

The findings came as a smack to many clergy and many experts of canons and Sacred Scripture, who did not so much preach a doctrine of geocentrism as take it for granted. On the evening of February 24, 1616, Galileo's "problem" was decided by a group of eleven scholars, none with mathematical expertise or a special interest in astronomy. The council ruled that Galileo's claims were not in agreement in Scripture or the Fathers, and should be treated, at least, as erroneous in faith.

The pope then asked the most trusted scholar and apologist of the day to deliver the news. Cardinal Robert Bellarmine presented the findings of the council to Galileo on February 25, 1616. This is the way St. Robert Bellarmine lived his life: humble, obedient, and willing to act upon the truths and decisions of the Catholic Church without hesitation.

Out of the thirty-six saints who have been declared Doctors of the Church, four of them were key players in the Counter-Reformation. Bellarmine is regarded by many as the most learned Catholic scholar in his time, and as the history of the Church shows, his superiors did not let his talent for apologetics and repute for debate go to waste. Complementary to his mastery of Church teaching and unmatched communication skills, Bellarmine had a tacit character of meekness and love. The meeting of these made for one of the most effective reformers of which the Church was truly in need: a brilliant, fearless, and gentle exponent of authentic Catholic teaching.

The Makings of a Reformer

Bellarmine's family of origin, from the Tuscan town of Montepulciano, was not wealthy but *was* well-connected in the Church. His uncle, the influential Cardinal Marcello Cervini, subsidized an education for young Robert in a school that matched his wits. In 1555, Cervini was elected pope, and all the Catholic Church believed that he would ring in great reforms. Though the Bellarmine family had high hopes, it would not be so. Pope Marcellus II's pontificate lasted only a month before he died. Still, soon Bellarmine discerned his own vocation to the priesthood.

Although his father wanted him to use his talents in a secular field, his mother encouraged him toward religious life. As an apparent answer to his mother's prayers, the Jesuits opened up a school in Montepulciano. Professors of nearly every discipline in the area wanted Robert as their pupil, but the new Jesuit school had a certain advantage: tuition was free. And so, within six months of attendance, near-constant study, and frequent conversing with the religious brothers, Robert had his mind made up: he was to go to Rome to become a member of the Society of Jesus. History records that he became one of the greatest members of that order: a scholar and apologist of godly character and just the sort of reformer the Church needed then—and needs again today. Historian James Hitchcock calls him the greatest and most influential theologian of his time,[82] which is why, in 1598, at the ceremony in which he became a cardinal, Pope Clement VIII said of him, "We elect this man because he has no equal for learning in the Church of God."[83]

Apologist

Bellarmine's interests and involvement in dogma reached beyond the demands of a learned priest. His abilities were extraordinary: he had a photographic memory, able to memorize an hour-long lecture, word for word, by reading it over once. His writings are numbered in the thousands, some still awaiting translation from his delicate Latin. The list of his accomplishments has no equal in his time. His catechism has been translated into sixty-two languages, everywhere from China to Peru. He aided his popes in the creation of textbooks and manuals on doctrine, assisted in the establishment of the Gregorian calendar, and served as a theological ambassador to straighten the civic and ecclesial errors of Venice,

France, Spain, and England. The credentials and achievements go on, and during all of this, his peers and disciples
testify that he spent hours in prayer every day, despite his poor
health since his childhood, and was among the most likeable
men they'd ever met.[84]

He also had the utmost respect of his Protestant challeng-
ers. It could be said that apologists are not just measured in
their effect on those with matching persuasions, but also with
the esteem and regard of their opponents. He was, indeed,
the authority any Protestant theologian would attempt to
debate or correct. Richard Montagu, Bishop of Chichester,
said of Bellarmine:

> He was a man, I must say, of wonderful industry and
> learning, and his reading was stupendous. He was the
> first and only one to put his hand with amazing skill
> to that shapeless mass of huge chaos of controversies, to
> reduce its confusion to order, and to give it elegance.
> And all this was done carefully and accurately after
> years of study. Outdistancing every rival, he snatched
> away the palm and won for himself all the praise in
> the world. Those who treat of controversies in our day
> borrow practically all their material from his stores, as
> the poets do from Homer.[85]

The vociferous Thomas Bell said that Robert is the man
"who hath said all that can be said for popery, and whose
testimony alone is most sufficient in all Popish affairs."[86]

Though his abilities were no doubt a gift from God, it
should be noted that his knowledge of the Faith was not
gained from an inward feeling of personal achievement, as
if he aimed for such a plateau, studied, and worked to get to
that mark. Rather, his success in scholarship derived from
two key areas: his ambition to do everything to the best of

his abilities, and his desire to defend and serve the Church. He did whatever was asked of him with impeccable skill and consistency in study and communication. The combination of these defining characteristics made him an apologetic force to be reckoned with.

Robert always did his best because he was *hungry for the truth*. What is the lesson for us? If we want to explain and defend the Faith effectively, we must be *lifelong learners*. There is no "easy button." Our study is not seasonal. Now, it took years of study before Bellarmine was ordained, and decades more for the full flowering of his powers. So we, too, must be patient. But we also must stay active in constant study. Bellarmine frames this notion perfectly: "Flee idleness, for no one is more exposed to such temptations than he who has nothing to do."[87]

With that noted, there are three other key imitations we can make of Bellarmine's scholarly life. First, we can surround ourselves with other scholars. Second, we can teach others in order to become masters of our field. Third, we can study the Faith and in tandem with ideas that contradict it.

Robert Bellarmine had an important habit of *surrounding himself with other learned people*. He understood the value of community in learning. Despite their own lack of advanced education, his parents must have made certain they ingrained in young Bellarmine the proper role of education. No doubt, this influenced him to include strong words when instructing other parents on their role as promoters of education:

> The generation of children, together with their proper education, must be had in view, if we would make a good use of matrimony . . . Again, it is a most grievous sin, for people united in matrimony and blessed with children, to neglect them or their pious education, or to allow them to want the necessaries of life.[88]

Robert took this lesson with him through his whole life. He was encouraged to join the Dominican brothers and priests in Montepulciano for conversation as often as he could spare. Years later, when the Society of Jesus opened a school in Montepulciano, Robert's mother ensured he was immediately enrolled. What a joy this must have been to the young and eager learner. He realized at an early age that an organized community of scholarship was his best preparation for serving the Church, and becoming a great apologist.

There's a proverb that says your character becomes a combination of the five people you are around the most. However true this is, exactly, no one can doubt the power of influence, and Robert certainly recognized it.

What, then, is the best way to surround ourselves with a community of scholars? There are many solutions but we will look at three.

The first is a third order. These are religious orders that allow laymen to participate in their spiritual tradition. Where the first order of the Dominicans, for example, is made up of ordained priests, and the second order of consecrated religious men and women, its third order is made up of laity who live in the world yet still wish to be formed in the Dominican tradition of a specific order. These are also sometimes referred to as *lay* or *secular* orders. Varieties of third order communities exist almost everywhere. They all feature a structured track for formation and prayerful living in the tradition of the order's founder.

Another kind of community in which most of us can seek scholarly fellowship is in Catholic groups found in colleges. There are numerous groups associated with authentic Catholic schools in which students may seek spiritual and academic knowledge, converse and bond with like-minded Catholics, and challenge one another to become better disciples. Even if you're not an enrolled student you can often find ways to participate in a college's Catholic academic community: through talks, debates, book clubs, study groups, and so on.

A final suggestion is to seek scholarly community on the internet. Online community can be accessed at any time from any place, making it convenient and giving each member enough time to carefully consider the conversation. Through the wonders of digital communication, we're able to correspond with the highest quality apologists, theologians, commentators, and thinkers of our day with a few simple clicks.

Wherever you seek intellectual community, always make sure you are learning from people you want to emulate. Make certain that there is an authentic Catholic culture present. And above all, confirm that orthodox views are being exchanged and presented.

Bellarmine's second secret to success was to become a *master apologist through becoming a teacher*. If you want to learn, you must study, but if you want to become a master, teach!

Young Robert chose the Jesuit order because it was created for the purpose of raising the most learned defenders of the Faith in the conquest of defeating heresies, primarily Protestant ideas. To do this, priests belonging to the Society of Jesus were required to be teachers. The reason for this rule is simple: all teachers are leaders, and all leaders are teachers.

In this respect, Bellarmine's desire to be a lifelong learner was bolstered by this desire to be a lifelong teacher. We must learn from this. Even though most of us will not become professors at a university, there are three areas in which most everyone can become a teacher: the family, the world, and the parish.

Those with families also fall into the broad category of teaching. For those who are called to a vocation in marriage and parenthood, a primary duty is to catechize children and to be sure they grow up in the Faith. Parents are not just called to *know* what the Church teaches but to *live* what the Church teaches. By ensuring our children are properly catechized and morally shaped, we ensure the next generation of Christians are equipped to handle challenges to their beliefs. Robert calls out the primary duty of parents:

> The generation of children, together with their proper education, must be had in view, if we would make a good use of matrimony.[89]
>
> Again: it is a most grievous sin, for people united in matrimony and blessed with children, to neglect them or their pious education, or to allow them to want the necessaries of life.[90]

Teaching that occurs in a family is not one-way, as all parents know. They often remark of the way their children "teach" them patience, among other things. Virtues can be developed, even if not formally taught. Similarly, spouses often teach each other a great deal. When they bring together their common interest in raising well-mannered and educated children, with their ability to communicate with and support each other to this end, spouses may become one of the most impactful teachers in our adult life. Therefore, the family unit is one of constant opportunity for teaching.

The secular world, where we live out our day-to-day life, if full of teaching opportunities as well. We can teach and witness to our neighbors, our co-workers, our larger community. The fathers of Vatican II, in the document *Apostolicam Actuositatem* (*Decree on the Apostolate of the Laity*), put it this way:

> They exercise the apostolate in fact by their activity directed to the evangelization and sanctification of men

and to the penetrating and perfecting of the temporal order through the spirit of the gospel. In this way, their temporal activity openly bears witness to Christ and promotes the salvation of men. Since the laity, in accordance with their state of life, live in the midst of the world and its concerns, they are called by God to exercise their apostolate in the world like leaven, with the ardor of the spirit of Christ.[91]

The parish, naturally, is a perfect place to teach as well. It is a microcosm of God's kingdom. Here we have a tremendous opportunity to serve others and be served. We attend Mass, we take children to be baptized, we celebrate lives and offer condolences at funerals and wakes, receive forgiveness for our sins, and we adore Christ in the Eucharist. Each Catholic, through parish life, has the ability and privilege to also teach or attend a Bible study, a men's or women's support group, or just to talk and grow with a priest or other spiritual mentor.

Those who preach and teach in the parish have an astoundingly important role in the development of souls. Robert instructs those who serve in the Church:

> I admonish and exhort all ecclesiastics, that being dead to the world, they live for God alone; not desiring an abundance of riches, zealously preserving their innocence, and assisting at divine things with devotion, as they ought, and endeavoring to make others do the same. Thus will they gain great confidence with God, and at the same time fill the Church of Christ with the good odor of their virtues.[92]

There are many opportunities to become a teacher, but it is necessary that all teachers be formed properly before they begin to instruct others in matters of formation, whether intellectual or religious. After all, all teachers are leaders, and that means that in some measure, all students are eventually fashioned in the character and thought of their instructor. It is, therefore, paramount that teachers maximize their effort to become prefect specimens of the gospel. Bellarmine commands the following:

> Three things are necessary for the attainment of the preacher's ends, three qualities of the soul without which his efforts will be unavailing. They are a great, vehement zeal for the honor of God, wisdom and eloquence. The fiery tongues which appeared above the apostles when God made them the first preachers of his Evangel are the symbols of these things: the burning fire, betokening zeal; the light, wisdom; and the form of a tongue, eloquence. Eloquence without charity and wisdom is only empty chattering. Wisdom and eloquence without charity are dead and profitless. And charity without wisdom and eloquence is like a brave man unarmed.[93]

Apologists will be manifestly successful if they surround themselves with scholars, and attempt teaching what they know to others, but *what they study* is also important. Robert's study was unique. There were others before him who studied to become scholars of Scripture, and others who became great students of the Church Fathers. Robert, though, became a broad-minded student of many disciplines in the intellectual tradition of the Church. He tied together deep understanding of Church history, Sacred Scripture, patristics, science, and philosophy to become a multidisciplinary apologist.

There was another major subject of learning that Bellarmine bravely ventured into, and that was the teachings of heretics and those anathematized. The way he saw it, there was no greater means of defeating false ideas than to truly understand them. This is the key to how Bellarmine became the model apologist, and his superiors in Rome knew that, even creating a new department of study purposed for him to chair: *controversial theology.*

His diverse knowledge along with his debate and negotiation skills made him a valuable ambassador. Pope Sixtus V employed him in handling the dilemma with (Protestant claimant to the throne of France) Henry of Navarre. Pope Paul V put his skills to use to fix a political situation with the Republic of Venice, and Bellarmine later became the theological adviser to Pope Clement VIII, handling another set of affairs political and religious.

The lesson is this: those who want to be an apologist on any level must be committed to studying several subjects with enthusiasm and efficiency, especially those ideas they intend to correct. Robert notes:

> To obtain the zeal or apostolic wisdom which is the very foundation of Christian preaching, nothing avails so much as assiduous prayer, constant and serous meditation, and the careful reading of spiritual books, especially such as contain the lives of the saints.[94]

Meek and Humble in Prayer

In addition to these three ways all of us can learn from and imitate St. Robert Bellarmine, there is a piece that sews them together, without which the entire garment would fall apart. In order to be an effective communicator of the Faith, whether as apologist, theologian, catechist, or preacher, two qualities must be present: meekness and humility. It's a fact of life that nobody is going to listen to you if you treat them like a jerk or are a complete hypocrite.

After having explained to Peter the difference between what we owe to God and what we owe to Caesar, Jesus was asked to explain who is the greatest in the kingdom of heaven. This topic and his answer, are not unrelated to the same lesson of giving Caesar what is Caesar's and to God what is God's:

> At that time the disciples came to Jesus, saying, "Who is the greatest in the kingdom of heaven?" And calling to him a child, he put him in the midst of them, and said, "Truly, I say to you, unless you turn and become like children, you will never enter the kingdom of heaven. Whoever humbles himself like this child, he is the greatest in the kingdom of heaven" (Matt. 18:1-4).

Humility and meekness are preconditioned assets to the success of the Catholic apologist, and each Catholic should learn them. They are what separate learned men and women from *great* men and women. You could acquire all the knowledge in the world and accomplish absolutely nothing without meekness and humility. Robert tells us:

> Therefore, we must first of all appeal to the minds of those who listen to us, and endeavor by sound reasons deduced from Holy Writ, by arguments of common sense, by examples and by similes, so to convince them that they will be forced to acknowledge the ideal of living which we propose as the only one becoming a reasonable man. Then by our eloquence and earnestness, and all the aids which rhetoric affords, we must endeavor to waken in their hearts a serious desire for that which their reason has already approved.[95]

Bellarmine would not have been a successful apologist without the eloquence and tact with which he wrote and spoke. To become the apologists that people *want* to listen to, our words and life must be imbued with the love of Christ. Bellarmine puts it this way: "Charity is that with which no man is condemned, without which no man is saved."[96]

In humility and meekness, the time a budding apologist and theologian spends in study must be one of devotion, prayer, and charity. What we study is, at the very least, equally important to how much we study. Offering encouragement to those involved in higher education, Bellarmine said to the student body while teaching at Louvain University in Belgium:

> Who is there in this illustrious home of learning who does not think daily as he goes to the schools of law, medicine, philosophy or theology, how best he may progress in his particular subject and win at last his doctor's degree? The school of Christ is the school of charity. On the Last Day, when the general examination takes place, there will be no question at all on the text of Aristotle, the aphorisms of Hippocrates, or the paragraphs of Justinian. Charity will be the whole syllabus.[97]

Bellarmine made a similar statement in his inaugural address as the Chair of Controversial Theology at Roman College in 1576:

> Our concern will not be with little things that make no difference however they stand, not with the subtleties of metaphysics, which man may ignore without being any the worse for it, but with God, with Christ, with the Church, with the sacraments, and with a

multitude of other matters which pertain to the very foundations of our faith.[98]

Make no mistake about it: an apologist will be without an audience unless he communicates with humility and meekness. And in order to achieve these, he must be devoted to prayer and love for the one he is informing. Don't know what to pray for? That's okay. A well-known youth who was given spiritual direction from Bellarmine remarked:

> [Humility] does not grow in our garden, but we must beg it from heaven . . . have recourse to the intercession of those saints who have excelled in this virtue . . . If you want to obtain a promotion in the army from an earthly prince, you would address him through the General of his forces or through one of the colonels, rather than through the Master of the Household, or any other domestic official. In the same way, if you wish to obtain fortitude from God, you would go to the martyrs for penance, to the confessors, and so with the rest.[99]

This young sage was none other than St. Aloysius Gonzaga, whom we will read about next.

Conclusion

St. Robert Bellarmine was a reformer to be reckoned with. He accomplished so much and made a huge impact on the Counter-Reformation. He worked to reverse anti-Catholic laws in Venice and England, produced the first post-Trent catechism, and fathered modern apologetics with hundreds of letters, books, and oral treatises. Countless are his contributions, but stringing together each of these was his softer touch in handling his opposition, the way he loved his mother

Church and the Jesuit Order, and most of all, for doing seemingly anything that was asked of him.

Becoming like Bellarmine might seem like moving a mountain, but the man who moves a mountain begins by carrying away small stones. We don't have to become masters of dogma overnight, or win over cities with our compassion at the snap of a finger. To become a scholar, start small: read often, converse with like-minded people you can look up to, and enroll in colleges or other institutions of learning where the Catholic faith and good philosophy are never taken lightly. Learning to become selfless and humble takes its roots in prayer and fasting, wherein we contemplate the simple life of Christ and the saints, and ask God to make us second and last in everything. We aren't supposed to look on ourselves with low value, rather, we are called to look on others with higher value. By adopting this simple worldview, we can really reform those around us.

If you would like to learn more about this model apologist, you should pick up the book *St. Robert Bellarmine*, which highlights his accomplishments and summarized his teaching on holiness. For a more complete biographical reading, you'll want to get a copy of *St. Robert Bellarmine: Saint and Scholar* by James Brodrick. There is also a short and useful biography I wrote in 2016, *St. Robert Bellarmine*. His writings can hardly be counted, but if you're in search of his best works on apologetics, make sure to get the volumes of *The Controversies*.

Prayer to St. Robert Bellarmine

O God, who adorned blessed Robert, the bishop and doctor, with marvelous learning and virtue to expose the deceptions of error and to defend the rights of the Apostolic See, grant by his merits and intercession, that love for the truth may increase in us, and the souls that do wander may return to the unity of thy Church. Through our Lord Jesus Christ, your Son, who lives and reigns with you in the unity of the Holy Spirit, one God, for ever and ever.

Chapter 5

St. Aloysius Gonzaga
Reformer of Youthful Piety

March 9, 1568–June 21, 1591
Feast Day: June 21

"I am but a crooked piece of iron, and have come into religion to be made straight by the hammer of mortification and penance."

What do you do when you're four years old and your dad is a marquis in the sixteenth-century Spanish army? You get your own toy gun and almost blow your hand and face off. What do you do when you're punished for it? You regain your repute by sneaking out to set off cannons in the middle of the night. That's exactly where we find our little prince, Aloysius Gonzaga, in the mid-1560s.

Aloysius—whom everyone referred to with love as "Luigi"—was between four and six years old when his father, Ferdinand, looked into the eyes of his sweet boy with the intent of making a good soldier out of him. He found a way to convince his wife Martha to let him take the boy to war in Tunis, Africa, in order to kindle his courage. Little Luigi was happy to practice loading and firing his tiny weapon. He gained the admiration of the burly soldiers and it didn't hurt to be the son of the commander. When the toy pistol misfired, causing the weapon to explode in his face, Aloysius was unharmed but considered himself disgraced.

Convinced that he needed to regain his reputation and respect, he snuck off to the other side of the camp to steal some powder and ammo from the supply. He carefully loaded the nearby heavy cannon and fired it. The entire camp awoke in confusion, thinking an enemy was inside the camp. Rushing to the scene armed with his men, Ferdinand found not only that it was his son who had fired the cannon, but that the recoil had not harmed him. The boy went unpunished only because the multitude of soldiers admired the little child and talked the marquis out of any further action.

Childlike Faith

If he was not a perfect child, St. Aloysius Gonzaga is nonetheless known to be one of the most pious, sinless examples of a Christian life, such that cause for his canonization was sought immediately after his death at just twenty-three. The life of a saint is supposed to consist of many great accomplishments, exemplary knowledge, obedience, sometimes martyrdom, sometimes miracles, and always heroic virtue. But few saints accomplish this all before they are grown and wise. Even fewer of those who are such prodigies of piety are world famous before their death. Our St. Aloysius has no equal in this regard.

The students of the class of 1892 of the College of St. Ignatius, New York City, made a mighty introduction to the young saint in their 1891 classic:

> Has a mighty general died? No! Has a learned philosopher or theologian passed away? No! Has a great orator or any of the lights of the world gone to eternal rest? No, none of these. Has a great hero died? Ah, yes! And that hero was but a young man.[100]

A reader might wonder why this saint so young is included with others involved in the Counter-Reformation. How much could he have accomplished in that effort? The Counter-Reformation had much to do with reforming the Church, apart from battling heresies. Heresies are infections in the Body of Christ, and the greatest heresy the Church suffered in the Reformation period was not Protestantism but the infection of self-love and corruption that crippled the Church's ability to accomplish its mission. Before the Church could actually reform, it needed to reform its heart—it needed great saints of virtue and love. Each of the saints of this period and movement were marked in this light, and truth be told, their works would not have amounted to much if they had no virtue or love. Aloysius wrote no books, had no enormous audiences, was not a martyr, and was no great philosopher or theologian. But he was more pious, blameless, penitent, and virtuously heroic than any other of his time. He was the model of the "childlike" faith to which all Christians are called.

So here is a Counter-Reformer who went from nearly killing himself before First Holy Communion to serving plague-stricken victims who would eventually infect and kill him. In every way possible, we have to admire and imitate his life. In this chapter we'll learn good qualities of his we can imitate along with some practical ways parents can cultivate these in their children. Then we'll unravel the arduous and sometimes antiquated practice—which Gonzaga would refer to as the key to any goodness in him—of holy mortifications and penances.

Obedience to Parents and to God

From his earliest days, the Marquis Ferdinand Gonzaga and his wife Isabel loved their son deeply, though their ambitions for Aloysius were drastically opposed. Ferdinand desired for his son and heir to become a great soldier and attendant to events in the king's court. Little Luigi was a prince, after all. Isabel, though, prayed for her son to realize a priestly or religious vocation. Caught in the middle of this was our future saint, on whom this marital disagreement would have significant effects. Indeed, if Aloysius did not have such a supernatural desire to follow God every bit that he was able, his religious vocation might have been threatened.

Parents must open their eyes to the perils of inconsistent guidance through example. If parents disagree about the Church and faith, the probability that a child will not go to church and leave their faith increases dramatically. Leave out visible disagreements and become passively disagreeable, and it can be even worse.

If one parent is faithful, making it to Mass every Sunday, but the other (particularly the father) is ambivalent, chances are high that the child will take up the ambivalence in later years.[101] Eventually, every child asks, "Why doesn't dad go to Mass?" or "Why do you both disagree about Christianity? Maybe I shouldn't even bother." The example parents set is paramount for the hope that their children will embrace a healthy faith.

As the world continues to fall into spiritual darkness, our children's faith and beliefs will be challenged ever more severely. They may even be mocked, punished, and persecuted. It becomes ever more incumbent for parents to be the beacons of wholesome goodness, stalwart defenders of the Faith, and unwavering examples of the conviction that the Faith demands. If we demand modern-day Counter-Reformers, we start with the parents!

The Vatican II document *Gravissimum Educationis* exhorts parents in this function of leadership and development:

Parents are the ones who must create a family atmosphere animated by love and respect for God and man, in which the well-rounded personal and social education of children is fostered. Hence the family is the first school of the social virtues that every society needs. It is particularly in the Christian family, enriched by the grace and office of the sacrament of matrimony, that children should be taught from their early years to have a knowledge of God according to the Faith received in baptism, to worship him, and to love their neighbor. Here, too, they find their first experience of a wholesome human society and of the Church. Finally, it is through the family that they are gradually led to a companionship with their fellowmen and with the people of God. Let parents, then, recognize the inestimable importance a truly Christian family has for the life and progress of God's own people.[102]

Isabel understood this principle. She dearly loved her husband and was submissive to him, but she was not a doormat. As a mother and a wife, she carried her cross by standing up for her son's religious development, and rightly protesting anything she believed put it in jeopardy. It is repeated by every biographer that she ensured that Luigi's first words were the names of Jesus and Mary, keeping his first joyful thoughts—even if they were mixed with those of toy guns—on religious zeal.

But there's a twist: Ferdinand, too, was a Catholic of deep religious conviction. Though he may have misread the religious potential of his son, his intention was never to prevent his son from loving and fearing God. We cannot just throw the marquis under the bus, but we must correct his course.

Ferdinand did not disrespect his wife, and in many biographical accounts we observe him listening to and acting upon her counsel. This is characteristic of a good leader. Where Ferdinand went wrong was when he doubted his wife's judgment and, at times, put his worldly concerns for Luigi above his divine calling. This is actually very common in saint stories, especially about the Counter-Reformers; fathers wanting to be completely sure of their son's vocation before giving up on their secular opportunities. St. Robert Bellarmine's father had the exact same concern, as did the father of Francis de Sales. Fathers of this time had prudent reason to be concerned about the future of their sons because they were heirs. As Ferdinand was a valued and respected member of the Spanish court, he had increased reason to be totally sure of the integrity of his household. A religious life is both very rewarding and very challenging, and when a son takes up religious vows he renounces all possessions and entitlements, which can potentially threaten the status of a family. Hindsight is always 20/20, so it is difficult to blame these fathers for not knowing the future sainthood of their sons.

King Philip of Spain also noticed the unique vocational talents of Gonzaga, having had the opportunity to question the young prince himself. One of his biographers speculated:

> Perhaps the tired and disheartened king, destined so soon to grow sadder still, more morose, more self-isolated, saw in the young man something that he took to resemble his own disgust with things and half-envied him the possibility of self-abdicating.[103]

Here's a rule all fathers can implement: always cultivate religious interests in your children, without exception. Even if they do not pursue a clerical or a religious vocation, they will have a solid Catholic foundation to hold them stable throughout their life. Here's an added suggestion for modern

fathers whose children show a seriousness for a religious vocation: along with listening to and considering the insight of
your spouse, make an effort to contact and use the expertise
of the vocations director in your diocese. To discern—or to
help your child discern—a religious vocation is to navigate
difficult and confusing waters, and expert help can be a
great aid.

Isabel and Ferdinand had in common deep religious conviction, a solid and loving marriage, and desire for the best
for their children. As we know, though, his father had been
annoyed by his son's aspirations. Our little saint knew this
and out of obedience took his father's orders when asked to
appear in court, but enjoyed none of it. Though he never
enjoyed it, he never pouted or showed hostility. He went so
far as to perfect the mannerisms of court life, not ignoring
the duties of his position.

There's a huge lesson for any young boy or girl (and still
some young adults in today's society) who wants to grow in
virtue and respectability. Part of true obedience—and something that will earn instant respect in any company—is not
just going along with instructions, but doing what must be
done to the very best of one's abilities. Though Aloysius took
the time to perform the duties requested by his father, he was
not without recreation in this period of his life as he spent
much time listening to and conversing with the local monks.
We have to find the right mixture of following God and
honoring our parents, even if the two seem to conflict. It's a
balancing act, but having a good attitude and keeping a lively
prayer life will assure us of God's hand in guiding our path.

Many of Aloysius's final letters were written to his family,
especially to his mother, who was still grieving the death of
his father and dealing with other stressful family issues re-
sulting from Aloysius's brother's new status as the marquis.

One such letter was written to his mother on the final day of 1590. He offered her a reminder of the identity of suffering available in reflecting on Jesus, and on Mary, too, which would have been of great comfort and solace to Isabel, who was going through so much. He writes:

> She is our real queen, from whose example we should receive better comfort than that offered by the queen of Spain, in whose service you are, or from anyone like her, who found herself in such a condition. So if it is a comfort to the afflicted, to have companions in like troubles, what greater consolation can your ladyship have than the company of Mary the virgin, as she who shares them with you is so great, and is in troubles and cares like those of your ladyship?[104]

Our saint truly loved and desired to honor his parents to the highest extent possible. A bittersweet moment completes this look at his obedient life and the deep love he had for his parents. Two months into his novitiate, he received word of the death of his father. Despite the news, he was happy to hear that prior to his death his father had performed works of penance and mercy, and died a happy death. Writing to his mother, "Now I may say—in a true and new sense—'Our Father, Who art in Heaven.'"[105]

Holy Mortifications

Could we imagine what it would be like if athletes stopped training their bodies? It would be unthinkable. Without training they would never have the strength and stamina required to perform. They also would lose their fans, since we respect athletes because of the great feats their training allows them to perform.

The same can be said of the saints, the champion athletes of the Faith. They are exemplars not of physical training but of the *ascetic life*. This ancient staple of our faith is viewed today by many as obsolete, superseded by our modern advances in . . . well that's just the problem. Nothing has filled the void of mortifications. For no reason other than an apparent ignorance and muted practice, we don't think much of penances unless it is those assigned to us after a confession, or a small pleasure we give up for Lent. We may be wearing the full armor of God, but it's paper thin. We're wielding spiritual swords, but against demonic temptations we're not even able to slice a stick of butter. Nothing has filled the void of mortifications because there is nothing that can. Mortifications and penances are the spiritual training that make us winners of the race, and winners of the good fight (2 Tim. 4:7).

In Scripture there are numerous references to mortification of the flesh but none is more clear (and more appropriate to compare to athletes) than Paul's exhortation to the Corinthians:

> Do you not know that in a race all the runners compete, but only one receives the prize? So run that you may obtain it. Every athlete exercises self-control in all things. They do it to receive a perishable wreath, but we are imperishable. Well, I do not run aimlessly, I do not box as one beating the air; but I pommel my body and subdue it, lest after preaching to others I myself should be disqualified (1 Cor. 9:24-27).

Paul is not sugarcoating his words here. To *pommel* literally means to strike and beat. There are amazing stories about the ways in which saints tamed their flesh. Saint Benedict is said to have jumped into a thorn bush to quit thinking lustfully. Philip Neri wore hot, itchy shirts made of horse hair. Saint

Gemma wore a thin belt of knots tightly under her clothes. And there's less severe mortifications performed by the saints, like when St. John Paul II slept on the floor. Mortifications are absolutely saintly because self-mastery is a requirement of every Christian.

Our saint, Aloysius Gonzaga, stands among the greatest of the self-mortifiers. The first reason he is an exemplar of mortification is his rigor, which is unmatched, and the second is his youth. "I am but a crooked piece of iron," he is popularly remembered as saying, "and have come into religion to be made straight by the hammer of mortification and penance."[106] We're going to draw a few lessons from him in order to encourage this holy obligation, and of strict importance, to do it the right way.

Aloysius correctly understood that mortifications were directed to self-denial and thus self-mastery. Another saying attributed to him that has come down to us is, "There is no more evident sign that anyone is a saint and of the number of the elect, than to see him leading a good life and at the same time a prey to desolation, suffering, and trials." But there seems to be no reason of the flesh that Gonzaga would *need* to mortify his flesh. He is regarded as one of the most sinless saints ever, which is why fellow Counter-Reformer St. Charles Borromeo rejoiced when he was privileged to serve Gonzaga his First Communion. He has been compared by saints of his generation and in later ones the best imitator of the child Jesus. Any further efforts at purity might seem to us like embellishment. Nonetheless, the wisdom of our young saint was so far beyond his years, and along with this he also had a teeming desire to suffer like the saints and martyrs he read so often about. But he was royalty and he was not going off to the dangerous adventures of a missionary any time soon. So as a means of participating like Peter and Paul in the sufferings of Christ (cf. Phil. 3:10; 1 Pet. 4:13), he continued this practice to share in this mystery.

What mortifications and penances did Aloysius perform, and what is necessary of us? Sometimes his mortifications left him bleeding three times per day. He was not shy of whipping himself, piercing his flesh, or sleeping with a plank of wood covering him. His fasting was to the extent that he considered eating just one egg to be a large meal. And his custody of his senses is noted in his constant avoidance of eye contact with women and anything that might cause temptation.[107] These are very strict, of course, and mortifications of this kind should *never* be performed without careful counsel from a spiritual director.

Mortifications and penances fall into three broad categories: physical exertions, fasting, and mental abstinences. Aloysius is well known, in addition to his rigor, for his variety and novelty in finding new ways to mortify himself. We want to do the same. The possibilities are almost endless, but here's some suggestions—drawn right from Aloysius's playbook—to get you started:

- *Physical Exertions:* stick a rock in your shoe, wear a tight belt, sleep with no pillow, maintain an off-season temperature in your house (if winter, have low heat; if summer, have little cooling), sleep with a piece of wood as a pillow, wear a hat with a tack in it.

- *Fasting:* no liquids other than water, eat tasteless food, abstain from meats, limited water intake, fast for one whole day a week, refuse fried/junk food, abstain from alcohol, abstain from soda/coffee/juices.

- *Mental Exertions:* wear unfashionable clothes, don't use your snooze button, pray in a perfect posture for a period of time, refrain from speaking to anyone (perhaps unless spoken to only), beg for money (and give proceeds to poor or parish), do not listen to secular music or indulge in other popular entertainment media.

This should be a healthy list to put you well on your way to a life of healthy mortifications. As you go on with these, and with some spiritual direction, you should be set to discover more variety and intensity.

Among all of these there was a certain penance that Aloysius held in disregard, one that made his blood quicken and his cheeks turn red at the thought; that was when he was praised for anything. For added results, do not pine for compliments and deny those that are given (try to place the merit on something or someone else). One item that helps us tame the flesh by way of taming our consciences is by decreasing our desire to be noticed, increasing our humility. To build this sense of un–identity, Aloysius performed some very humiliating acts. He would sometimes beg in a disguise (as Bellarmine and Neri did), and because of his popularity he relegated himself to be noticed as little as possible. He said:

> People who see me either know me, or they do not. If they do not know me, I ought not to care what they think; and if they do know me, I really lose none of their esteem; on the contrary, they may probably be edified, so that, in fact, there might be more danger of vain glory than of shame, for even the worldly often admire those who make themselves poor for the love of God.[108]

Often times, in this, he would beg and ask for things he knew he could not possibly obtain for the sole purpose of enduring a rebuke and humiliating rejection. Naturally, he would be asked by his peers why he went to such lengths. To them he recollects:

> The persons who give me this advice are of two sorts; some lead such holy and perfect lives that I can discern nothing in them but what is worthy of imitation, and I have more than once determined to abide by their counsels, but when I noted that they themselves did not observe them in their own conduct, I judged it better to imitate their action than to follow the recommendations, which through a certain charitable feeling and compassionate affection they give me. Others there are, who themselves do not follow the advice which they give me, and are not much addicted to penitential exercises; but I consider it better to rule myself by the example of the former than by the counsel of the latter.[109]

Aloysius is saying that he was more willing to follow the example of those he wanted to imitate as he became more and more spiritually mature, than the advice of the hypocrites. We should take his wisdom into deep consideration in every mortification and penance we consider.

One might expect this saint, so practiced in the art of mortification, to be touchy and irritable, perhaps crippled and constantly looking sore. He didn't, and he wasn't. Virgil Cepari, a Jesuit companion and later a biographer under the direction of Robert Bellarmine, noted:

> Whether he was sitting, talking, or standing his whole exterior was a perfect portrait of modesty: his face beamed with joyous serenity, which he communicated to those who beheld it. Never was he seen to change

his countenance in any circumstance, nor to lose his
tranquility, to become melancholy, or break out into
unrestrained gaiety. He was always the same, should
that his passions were under control and that he pos-
sessed an imperturbable inner peace and calmness: nor
was there ever seen in him the last sign of impatience
or anger . . . all his actions manifested his profound
humility.[110]

Conclusion

As we have seen, Aloysius is an extraordinary example of reform—of his own soul and those to whom he was an inspiring example—based on a life committed to mortification and
penance. His early life is a case study for the joys and the
challenges of Catholic parenting. He is also a patron saint of
youths. He reminds young men and women to be subject to
the rule of their parents, and he stands as stirring proof that
even teenagers and young adults can master both their flesh
and their spirit. As a fellow student of his once said, "I did not
want to come [to confession], I felt so much repugnance and
shame; but Aloysius urges me to come and it is he who brings
me here by main force."[111] Bellarmine, his confessor and spiritual director, said, "God has been pleased to exalt his young
servant that all young persons may know that youth is not an
obstacle to the attainment of mature virtue, and knowing this
may be animated by his example to seek after perfection."[112]

Reading and discovering more about this glorious patron saint of youths is highly encouraged, especially for little ones. Most books for young boys and girls include stories highlighting this saint, and the reader searching for a more robust biography should look no further than the classic by J.F.X. O'Conor, *Life of St. Aloysius Gonzaga of the Society of Jesus*, which has been quoted in this chapter several times. The motivated bibliophile will enjoy the rare out-of-print titles from Fr. Clifford Stevens of Boys Town, *Aloysius* and the title by Maurice Meschler S.J., *St. Aloysius Gonzaga: Patron of Christian Youth*.

Prayer to St. Aloysius Gonzaga

Dear Christian youth, you were a faithful follower of Christ in the Society of Jesus. You steadily strove for perfection while generously serving the plague-stricken. Help our youths today who are faced with a plague of false cults and false gods. Show them how to harness their energies and to use them for their own and others' fulfillment—which will redound to the greater glory of God. Amen.

O most glorious St. Aloysius, who has been honored by the Church with the fair title of "angelic youth," because of the life of utmost purity you led here on earth, I come before your presence this day with all the devotion of my mind and heart. O perfect exemplar, kind and powerful patron of young men, how great is my need of you! The world and the devil are trying to ensnare me; I am conscious of the arbor of my passions; I know full well the weakness of inconstancy of my age. Who shall be able to keep me safe if not you, O

saint of angelic purity, the glory and honor, the loving protector of youths? To you, therefore, I have recourse with all
my soul, to you I commit myself with all my heart. I hereby
resolve, promise, and desire to be especially devout toward
you, to glorify you by imitating your extraordinary virtues
and in particular your angelic purity, to copy your example,
and to promote devotion to you among companions. O dear
St. Aloysius, guard and defend me always, in order that, under your protection and following your example, I may one
day be able to join with you in seeing and praising my God
forever in heaven. Amen.

Chapter 6

Pope St. Pius V
Reformer of Faithful Leadership

January 7, 1504–May 1, 1572
Feast Day: April 30

*"All the evils of the world are
due to lukewarm Catholics."*

Popes usually don't win naval battles. Popes don't usually fight in wars at all, but Lepanto was more than a temporal battle. It was a spiritual struggle against the heresy of Islam; a monument to the resolve of Christian unity against a brutal common aggressor. And it was associated with the promises of the most holy rosary of the Blessed Virgin Mary. Pope St. Pius V stands at the center of this epic event.

Bl. John Henry Newman famously remarked of the historical clash:

The Turkish successes began in the middle of the XI century. They ended in the XVI. Selim the Sot came to the throne of Othman and Pt. Pius V to the throne of the apostle . . . The Battle of Lepanto arrested forever the danger of Mohamedan invasion in the South of Europe—and Lepanto was won by prayer.

There is no possibility in overstating the importance of Lepanto, or the sheer improbability of the victory won by the West. It ranks among the greatest events that shaped the course of the Church and history itself.[113] What Pius V accomplished in uniting the Christian West and having the courage to entrust the entire endeavor to Our Lady is a testament to his leadership, faith, and guile.

As all ship captains know, sometimes you have to turn into the tide in order to pursue a straight course. Pius V commanded and steered St. Peter's Barque with this boldness and faithful foresight, trusting in Christ and delegating his faculties to the supernatural when required. Without his leadership, there may have been no Counter-Reformation at all.

More Than a Pope

Few of us will be a pope, or a queen, or a military commander. But though we may never command a nation, all of us have to make choices that affect our state and way of life. We all have to *lead*: in our lives, our families, our business, even in our efforts to evangelize. For this we must be prepared. Pius V never thought *he* would be pope, but when he became pope, however reluctant he was, he was prepared to step up and steer the ship.

This preparation did not come from years of studying in Pope School. Pius was prepared because he opened himself to whatever God called him to, being completely obedient to God's will. Throughout his whole life, Antonio Ghislieri desired a small role in the kingdom, to be God's vessel for any use. He became a Dominican friar, taking the name Michele. There is so much to learn from Pius V, but in looking at him as a model for our own reform we will focus on two: his deep love for the Blessed Virgin Mary and his trust in the rosary, and his instinctive set of leadership skills.

Devotion to and Trust in the Rosary

Pope Pius V's résumé of accomplishments is impressive. It includes the reformation of the missal, the breviary, a catechism, and a complete restructuring of the seminaries and youth education by establishing the Confraternity of Christian Doctrine (CCD).[114] He instituted the Congregation of the Index, which created a list of books and writings viewed to be heretical.[115] His contributions to standardizing the Church and defending it from Protestant errors and Islamic conquest is truly extraordinary, especially given his short term in the Chair of Peter.

What enabled him to achieve so much in so short a time was his deep and contemplative prayer life and his typically Dominican desire to share those fruits with others. His Dominican prayer life included a devotion to the holy rosary, in the power and promises of which he placed his full trust. From the moments his health suffered to the hour when Western civilization itself was threatened, this trust extended to every aspect of his ministry and private life. He prayerfully remarked, "In union with the perfect confidence and hope that the Holy and Blessed Virgin placed in thee, do I hope O Lord."

There is a beautiful scene in *The Lord of the Rings* where Pippin the hobbit asks Gandalf whether there is any hope for his friends Frodo and Sam, sent on a dangerous mission to destroy the evil Ring of Power. "Just a fool's hope," Gandalf replies.

Gandalf was not saying the Frodo and Sam's errand was foolish. Rather, he was pointing out that hope, if it exists in any measure, is still hope. And even the smallest amount of hope—"a fool's hope"—is powerful enough to direct our path and win the war of souls. The apostles must have felt the same way. On the night of Jesus' arrest they understood exactly what the fate of their leader was, and once his death was confirmed they must have been tempted to despair in everything they learned. To the world, the Faith is foolish: we put our trust in a God who let himself be murdered in a humiliating way. Now we have been waiting for his return, which he said was imminent, for almost 2,000 years. According to the wisdom of the world, Christians are complete fools.

Pius V had a fool's hope in the rosary. In 1570, the Ottoman Empire made advances on large parts of the Christian West, brutalizing and enslaving Christians everywhere they went. They had their eyes set on conquering Europe. At the time, the Republic of Venice, the Spanish Empires, the Holy Roman Empire, the Papal States, France, and the kingdom of Naples and Venice had no desire for unity. They agreed that they didn't want the Islamic Turks to impose rule on Christian Europe, but they didn't know how to stop them. Leaderless, dispersed, and severely lacking in morale—they were nearly hopeless.

In September, the Turkish troops landed on the island of Cyprus and slaughtered 20,000 Christians within days. France intended to side with Elizabeth of England, who was in the process of negotiating a commercial treaty, believing that the pope was more interested in destroying Protestantism than driving away the Turks. Almost all hope had faded when Pius threw himself into prayer and fasting over the matter. By the summer of 1571, Pius was only able to gather the help of Spain, Venice, and Genoa and other Italian states, and appointed the young war strategist Don Juan to command the joint naval forces.

Two years earlier, Pope Pius V had written the Bull *Consueverunt Romani Pontifices* (*Accustomed to the Roman Pontiffs*), made the rosary an officially approved prayer and laid forth a universal way to pray this "Psalter of the Blessed Virgin Mary"—the same way it is prayed to this day—as a potent means of defeating heresy. His uncompromising words of instruction and endorsement read:

> For [the Glorious Virgin Mary, loving Mother of God] by her seed has crushed the head of the twisted serpent, and has alone destroyed all heresies, and by the blessed fruit of her womb has saved a world condemned by the fall of our first parent. From her, without human hand, was that stone cut, which, struck by wood, poured forth the abundantly flowing waters of graces. And so Dominic looked to that simple way of praying and beseeching God, accessible to all and wholly pious, which is called the rosary, or psalter of the Blessed Virgin Mary, in which the same most Blessed Virgin is venerated by the angelic greeting repeated 150 times, that is, according to the number of the Davidic Psalter, and by the Lord's Prayer with each decade. Interposed with these prayers are certain meditations showing forth the entire life of our Lord Jesus Christ, thus completing the method of prayer devised by the by the Fathers of the Holy Roman Church. This same method St. Dominic propagated... Christ's faithful, inflamed by these prayers, began immediately to be changed into new men. The darkness of heresy began to be dispelled, and the light of the Catholic faith to be revealed.

Following the example of our predecessors, seeing that the Church militant, which God has placed in our hands, in these our times is tossed this way and that by so many heresies, and is grievously troubled and afflicted by so many wars, and by the depraved morals of men, we also raise our eyes, weeping but full of hope, unto that same mountain, whence every aid comes forth, and we encourage and admonish each member of Christ's faithful to do likewise in the Lord.[116]

Leading by his own example, the pope sought a solemn pact that the rosary would be prayed daily and in full in the galley of each ship. Pius also ensured that Jesuit, Franciscan, and Dominican priests offered Mass on each ship daily, and that confessions were regularly heard. Pius was preparing for spiritual warfare; Catholic Don Juan was preparing the fleet for physical warfare.

Early in October, the Turks landed on Famagusta of Cyprus, overtook the city within hours, and flayed the commander alive, sending shockwaves of fear throughout the region. Now the two fleets were finally ready to meet, in a naval battle that would either repel the Ottoman invaders or leave them free to use the Mediterranean to run amok through Europe. Before the engagement, though, Pius V had made sure that the priests reminded the troops of the plenary indulgence available to those who faithfully give their life for the Lord, and Don Juan lifted high the reliquary the pope had provided.

That day, more than 7,500 Christian men united in the Holy League lost their lives, but the Turks lost everything, totaling 30,000 deaths and 8,000 captured.[117] Almost the entirety of the Turkish fleet had been powered by the muscle of Christian slaves, but those who survived were now freed. Back in Rome, the pope was going over finances when he suddenly arose from his study, approached the window facing east and tearfully said, "The Christian fleet is victorious."[118] Two weeks later, word of victory arrived by official courier. His vision was prophecy, and his instrument of success was a set of beads joined on a string.

Pius V trusted in the rosary because he had confidence in the Blessed Mother; he had confidence in her because God chose her, among all creation, to deliver himself for the salvation of all mankind. He believed that she continues, through her intercession, to bring the God's salvation to those who seek it.

We should do the same. Praying the rosary, like any other prayer, begins and ends with two balancing ideas: confidence and consistency. If we pray consistently, our confidence will grow. If we pray with confidence, we are surely going to pray more consistently.

It's not easy. As simple as the prayer is—so simple that children as young as two can learn the basic formula—it takes fortitude to pray the rosary consistently. Many a Catholic has resolved to pray the rosary every day only to find he can't go more than a few days without forgetting or getting distracted with other things. We've all looked at our rosary on our countertop or nightstand and told ourselves, "I need to pray that more," but cannot seem to reach any level of consistency. *I'm too tired, I need to sleep, I need to go to work, I lose concentration, I don't meditate on the mysteries, I don't know the mysteries, I always forget, I yawn a lot, I get bored with the repetition, I can't concentrate, my spouse will not pray with me, my roommate will think I'm weird, I don't like the rosary, I don't own a rosary, I can find my rosary . . .*

Some of these reasons are telling of how selfish we are with our time, some reveal of how undisciplined we are, and others may be signs that we're disillusioned with our faith. There's always a reason. The common thread is a lack of *consistency*.

The first step in being consistent with the rosary is to *ask God for the grace to pray it at all*. This might come as a shock to some, but yes, we must ask for graces from God to pray in order to obtain more graces through prayer. This is comforting, because we can immediately take the burden off ourselves and realize that we require grace to perform any and every good work. Paul told the church at Ephesus, "For by grace you have been saved through faith, and this is not your own doing; it is the gift of God" (Eph. 2:8). The *Catechism* puts it this way: "These graces and goods are the object of Christian prayer. Prayer attends to the grace we need for meritorious actions" (2010) and "Prayer is both a gift of grace and a determined response on our part. It always presupposes effort" (2725). Therefore, before we commit to praying the rosary every day, or once a week before Mass, we must ask God for help in doing so.

Next, *start small!* Jumping into the ocean before having the endurance to swim to shore is a terrible and deadly mistake. Just the same, thinking the only way to pray honorably is to commit to praying a lot, immediately, can do more harm than good. When Paul told the Thessalonians to pray without ceasing, he did not mean for them to ignore their worldly responsibilities or to otherwise zealously jump in the deep end. When Paul V told the commanders of the fleet to pray the rosary on every ship, he knew they also had a duty to train and prepare for battle.

Rather than committing to praying the rosary every day to start, try praying a single decade in the morning, or try sticking a rosary in your pocket and saying one Hail Mary every time you happen to reach in there. From that point, double up! Say another decade in the evening, or say one Hail Mary every hour on the hour. Soon, and this is a promise, it will become habitual once you see the benefits of focusing on God throughout your day; then you'll eventually *want* to pray the rest of the rosary.

After asking for the desire to pray and working our way up to regularly praying full prayers, we have to sustain this.

What's left in the development of a more consistent prayer life is the need to be *disciplined*. When we think of people who are disciplined, we think of rigid, orderly, focused, task-oriented people. That's a great visual, but disciplined people were not born with those characteristics; they *are disciplined* because they *were disciplined*. Discipline is a formative process that leads to a current state. Just as one cannot be a teacher without first being a student, one cannot be a disciple without first being disciplined; no discipline, no disciple.

This is perfectly represented in the disciples of Christ who would become the apostles of Christ. The Bible tells that there were a multitude who followed Jesus (Mark 2:5), but not all of these were really disciples. Some of them followed because he would feed them, and others because they wanted to see a great sign. But those we know as disciples were the ones who *learned from a master* (John 13:13). They didn't simply admire Christ; they were *devoted* to him!

What made them disciples? Jesus taught them, but they didn't just listen. *They left what they were doing in order to follow him.* Levi was working at a tax booth when he "got up and followed [Jesus]" (Mark 2:14). Peter, James, and John received his invitation and "left everything and followed him" (Luke 5:11). It was the same with each of the apostles and it is the same with us. When we receive the call to follow God, we must abandon our former lives. Now, to be clear, our "former lives" does not mean we have to leave our careers and our families (although it may for some). It means that we leave our *way* of life. Before, we might have spent hours and hours playing video games, significant amounts of money gambling, or time mulling over ways to get back at people who sin against us. This is the life we are leaving in exchange for a life of following Christ, where we will be disciplined by his Word. Just as a father disciplines his children when they are out of line, God disciplines us in order to form us according to his perfect will. Sometimes it's painful. Other times the burden is light.

Praying consistently is natural to this process. Instead of playing video games, we pray to, study about, and tell others about Christ. Instead of gambling high stakes, we generously give alms. Rather than holding grudges, we prayerfully forgive others. This discipline is refined by a life of prayer. The more we hope to follow Christ, the more we must be devoted to praying because praying aligns us with his perfect will, and praying the rosary is a specially powerful means of achieving that end.

Most people will not put forth this sort of priority. Most people are lukewarm, even most Catholics! St. Pius V tells us in straightforward words that, "all the evils of the world are due to lukewarm Catholics." Enough said.

Matching our consistency with the rosary, we must have great *confidence* in it as well. From the very early days of Christianity the faithful have venerated and asked for the intercession of the Blessed Virgin Mary. There is more than one tradition about the origins of the rosary, [119] but everyone can agree that the majority of the prayer is completely biblical. If, then, the rosary is supported by Scripture and events in history, there is no reason not to take up this mighty tool as a means to enrich our devotions to Jesus and his Blessed Mother. It was not because Pius V was Pius V that his rosary was efficacious. It didn't have anything to do with him being the vicar of Christ. The truth is, the rosary was instrumental in the Battle of Lepanto because of what the rosary *is*. It is more than a set of beads on a rope; it is the very representation of faith, hope, and love that centers our religion. In faith, we trust in God's Word. In hope, we believe his promises. In love, we devotedly work out our salvation by praying for others and ourselves. In a word, the rosary is our most practical devotion. By reflecting upon the life of the woman who was the tabernacle of Christ, suffered alongside the Son of Man, and completely submitted herself to God's will, we become the best disciples of Christ by following his first disciple—his mother.

Because of what the rosary is, when it was recited by tens of thousands of Christians before the imminent battle, their prayers of faith, hope, and love helped secure the victory of heaven and its citizens. Our ultimate confidence in the rosary is confidence in our Savior and imitating those who are the best examples of extraordinary faith, hope, and love.

Faithful Leadership

Change requires leadership, and the Catholic Church during the Reformation needed both. Pius V had a lot of work cut out for him when he became the bishop of Rome. The Council of Trent had been brought to a close by Charles Borromeo and his uncle Pius IV almost three years before. The council had accumulated many decrees and constitutions but there was no plan, yet, to organize and execute the reforms. It was a huge job, and the task required a leader who knew what to do and how to do it.

Pius V was not intimidated by any amount of work. He was stern, uncompromising, and bold long before he became pope. Where this era of the Catholic Church was filled with laxity and corruption, Michele Ghislieri had been meticulous in his rule, and was a staunch advocate of moral and doctrinal perfection.

Before he was pope he had become prior of several Dominican houses where he was known for his strict demands, but also for his unquestionable ability to live up to those demands himself. Those in power around him recognized this, and he was made an inquisitor, charged with identifying and correcting heresies. During the lifetime of Pius V, another saint who abhorred heresy was St. Francis de Sales, who laid out the task perfectly: "It is our duty to denounce as strongly as we can heretical and schismatic sects and their leaders. It is an act of charity to cry out against the wolf when he is among the sheep, wherever he is."

Once when Pius was reproached by a cardinal for his severity, he replied, "Nothing can be too severe for those who attempt to hinder the ministers of religion in their rightful duties." It was not out of hate, for Pius V was loved by many. It was not out of spite, for he was supported by those he opposed. And it was certainly not out of selfishness, because he never gained from any of his strictest orders. Pius V was the leader he was because he knew what worked. He also knew how to use power effectively but not unjustly, and how to vary his leadership style to the situation. In fact, he mastered no fewer than *five* leadership styles, each of which is instructive for us today.

The first leadership style Pius V exemplified was the *authoritative style*. This is the least enjoyable of all the styles to experience, because this is the leader who says, "This is how we're going to do it, and you're either on board or you're not." The authoritative leader is what you want when quick and compliant results are necessary. People can handle "crisis mode" for only so long, though, so this method of leadership has to be used sparingly and when the benefits *really* outweigh the cultural risks.

One of the first things he did when he became pope was to dismiss—why it was there to begin with, I don't know—the papal court jester. If he wanted to be taken seriously, he had to take his office, literally his office, seriously. A more substantive example of authoritative leadership we can identify in his pontificate was his revision of the missal. It was no small or easy reform, and his success in pulling it off testifies to his talent as an authoritative leader.

This leader must have superior self-control to ensure that he does not abuse his power, alienate others, or fail to recognize input from proper channels. As with the other leadership styles but especially the authoritative style, the leader must himself observe the level of scrutiny he demands of others. He cannot be a hypocrite. In every case, Pius V lived up to the demands he gave others. When he ordered the galley commanders to pray the rosary every day, he did, too. When he told the king of France that one may never do evil on order to accomplish good, our saint held himself to the highest moral standards. The authoritative style only works if the leader can walk the walk and talk the talk.

Next is the *visionary style* of leadership. This is the leader who knows how to motivate people to understand and be enthusiastic about their goal. Rather than "do it my way," this leader says, "Let's do this together," and understands the principle of delegation. Here, the leader sets the "big picture" rules but execution may occur at the lowest levels possible.

The Church is in many ways visionary with its tradition of subsidiarity. Another Pope Pius—the eleventh—would write about it in an encyclical:

> Just as it is gravely wrong to take from individuals what they can accomplish by their own initiative and industry and give it to the community, so also it is an injustice and at the same time a grave evil and disturbance of right order to assign to a greater and higher association what lesser and subordinate organizations can do. For every social activity ought of its very nature

to furnish help to the members of the body social, and never destroy and absorb them.[120]

The visionary leader has to have clear vision and positivity. He must be able to motivate others by his own energy and enthusiasm. Pius V used the traits of a visionary leader to accomplish other reforms. His revision of the breviary and the catechism, for example, each required the ability to motivate others to "buy in" on the idea and execute its completion.

Another style of leadership is the *coaching style*. The coach is the leader who is interested in developing people for the future. He is able to see and correct shortcomings, and also to maximize the talents of others. After reading about his strictness, few might believe that Pius V was a good coach. In fact, all leaders, to some extent, must be good coaches, and Pius V was among the best. Even before he was pope, as a priest and pastor of souls, he was most interested in the well-being and development of his peers and subordinates, but especially the laity.

He was called upon to assist in the dealings of Sixtus of Siena, a young and bright Franciscan friar whose popular sermons were discovered to be tainted with heresy. Being released after proper correction and swearing not to return to his persuasion, he eventually fell back to preaching the heretical ideas. Rather than giving a total reprimand, Pius approached him in friendship, promising that he would help him see past his errors and continue to live a saintly life. In time, Sixtus repented fully and was reinstated to the priesthood and readmitted to the black and white of the Dominican order.

Coaching requires being a role model. Pius V was able to get the most out of people because he was convincing, and more so because he was the sort of person people *wanted* to imitate. He also had the patience required of his style. Coaching requires a lot of focused work in the present for benefits that will only occur in the distant future. Sometimes the coach may never see the fruits of his work.

Another important method of leadership is *democratic style*. The democratic leader enables change and action through gaining consensus and participation. The democratic leader asks, "How would *you* do it?" He leads a team in which everyone has an opportunity for input. The benefits of this style are trust and transparency, as well as the unique mix of personal responsibility and team commitment.

There's an example in Pius V when he had a desire to reform the art in churches and other sacred locations. Popes prior to him enjoyed the recent Renaissance art and others used ornate pieces as a means of displaying power. Pius V was more ambivalent on the subject and only wished for the end state to reflect more reverence for God and the service to truth and the Christian religion. In order to do this he called on some experts (and future saints): Philip Neri and Charles Borromeo. Together, the reforms were agreeable and the implementation was a success. The achievement was so successful that the work on the new St. Peter's Basilica continued, and it was assured that the team produced architects and artists who understood there wasn't to be a single deviation from the original design and intent of Michelangelo.

A final leadership style exhibited by Pius V is the *expressive style*. This is the style of the "people's leader": the leader who forms authentic relationships and builds respect from empathy. This style seeks success by working through.

Due to his shrewdness there were many times where Pius V was opposed, and many other times when he had to oppose others. One such instance, when he was a cardinal, is found in his relations with Pius IV, his predecessor and the pope who gave him the red hat and made him general inquisitor. Then-Cardinal Ghislieri took issue with Pius IV's attempt to make a cardinal of his thirteen-year-old nephew. Though he was known to speak out in firmness, here our saint did so knowing he could lose favor. Still, he did what he knew to be correct, and objected with firm tact. He did win the argument. But something special happened when he was backed in the matter by another papal nephew: Charles Borromeo. Before Ghislieri had even left the papal court following the dispute, Pius IV died. In the subsequent conclave, likely with influence from Borromeo, who respected him, Antonio Ghislieri was elected pope.

All leaders are responsible for managing change because change is inevitable. There are many things about the Church that are immutable, but the Church will always have the challenge of responding to the changing world around it. Great leaders respond to change with the style appropriate for the situation and outcome. Pius V understood how to harness and use his abilities in order to allow the Holy Spirit to work through him for the preservation and reformation of the Church. His leadership qualities are each worth meditating upon and imitating.

Conclusion

Pius V was anything but lukewarm, and nothing less than rigid. He held himself to a very high standard of living and discipline. He held back nothing in order to do what God asked of him, and although he never wanted to be anything more than a simple priest, he reminded himself that he was God's servant first and that his primary responsibility was preparing himself to be that vessel for the Holy Spirit.

Like any good friend and pastor of souls, Pius V did his best to inspire this standard of life in those around him. Through his fidelity to Christ and trust in the rosary, he became a saint.

Not all popes, even those who were saints, have a lot of extant quotes or works. Though he was a preacher in the Order of Preachers, there are few words and works available for those looking for deeper reflection. Students of the saints who want to read more from and about Pius V will find some success orienteering the internet for a small amount of his papal bulls, but generally limited and incomplete content. A popular biography to read is from Robin Anderson. It is a gem and a quick read. Lovers of history must listen to *The Battle of Lepanto* by Christopher Check.

There is no liturgical or recognized devotional prayer to Pope St. Pius V, but I like to think we all already know his devotional prayer: *the holy rosary*. Most Catholics know how to pray the rosary, but few realize that the Dominican rosary is just slightly different. In order to honor the memory of our Dominican pope, here is the Dominican rosary.

1. Make the *Sign of the Cross.*
   V. "Hail Mary full of grace, the Lord is with thee."
   R. "Blessed art thou among women and blessed is the fruit of thy womb, Jesus."
   V. "O Lord, open my lips."
   R. "And my mouth shall declare your praise."

    V. "O God, come to my assistance."
    R. "O Lord, make haste to help me."

2. "Glory be to the Father, and to the Son, and to the Holy Spirit. As it was in the beginning is not and will be forever. Amen. Alleluia." (omit "alleluia" during Lent)

3. Say ten *Hail Marys* after announcing the first mystery; meditate on each mystery throughout each respective decade.

4. Say the *Glory Be.* (The Dominican rosary does not use the Fátima prayer, "O my Jesus...")

5. Announce the next Mystery; Say the *Our Father.*

Repeat three through five (above) for the second, third, fourth, and fifth mysteries.

Concluding prayers

Hail, holy queen, mother of mercy, our life, our sweetness and our hope! To thee do we cry, poor banished children of Eve; to thee do we send up our sighs, mourning and weeping in this valley of tears. Turn, then, most gracious advocate, thine eyes of mercy toward us, and after this our exile, show unto us the blessed fruit of thy womb, Jesus. O clement, O loving, O sweet Virgin Mary!

    V. Queen of the most holy rosary, pray for us.
    R. That we may be made worthy of the promises of Christ.
    V. May the divine assistance remain always with us.
    R. And may the souls of the faithful departed through the mercy of God, rest in peace. Amen.

Let us pray. O God, whose only begotten Son, by his life, death and resurrection, has purchased for us the rewards of eternal life, grant we beseech thee, that meditating on these mysteries of the most Holy rosary of the Blessed Virgin Mary, we may imitate what they contain and obtain what they promise, through the same Christ, Our Lord. Amen.

Chapter 7

St. Philip Neri
Reformer of Solemn Humor

July 21, 1515—May 25, 1595
Feast Day: May 26

"A prayer for peace."
(St. Philip Neri's recommendation for an after-wedding prayer)

By early middle age, the average man of the sixteenth century could generally figure where the rest of his life was going. When he was thirty-five, though, Philip Neri didn't have a clue.

At that time he had a stake in returning to his family business, he had already made advanced studies in Rome, and he had a growing followership for his abundant holiness and charismatic personality. But maybe he would live the rest of his life in a solitary state? Philip was unsure of this calling, unconfident that a life as a recluse would bring the greatest glory to God.

So Philip prayed, fervently, for God's will. His following grew, traveling with him to and from churches, praying when he prayed, resting when he rested, and when Philip was ready, they would listen to his homiletic preaching. But Philip continue to pray.

Around this time, in the year 1550, while praying and meditating, he received a miraculous visitation from John the Baptist. Philip had been baptized in the church of John the Baptist in his hometown of Florence, and, like John, was accustomed to an austere lifestyle—performing mortifications and regularly acting out in embarrassing ways as to increase his humility. Suddenly there was no more uncertainty in Philip. When the biblical martyr told him, "The will of God for you, Philip, is that you should pass your life in the midst of the city as if in a desert," he knew at once what that meant.

From here on, like John the Baptist, Philip knew his life's mission was to apply himself to the conversion of other people's hearts and personal holiness, not just his own. How he went about doing that was a combination of holiness, irony, and contradiction, making him a unique saint of solemn humor.

The Holy Humorist

When Philip Neri walked abroad
Beside the Tiber, praising God,
They say he was attended home
By half the younger set of Rome.
Knight, novice, scholar, boisterous boy,
They followed after him with joy.
To nurse his poor and break his bread
And hear the funny things he said.
For Philip Neri (by his birth
A Florentine) believed in mirth,
Holding that virtue took no harm
Which went with laughter arm-in-arm.
Two books he read with most affection—
The Gospels and a joke collection;
And sang hosannas set to fiddles
And fed the sick on soup and riddles.
So when the grave rebuke the merry,

Let them remember Philip Neri.
(Fifteen-fifteen to ninety-five),
Who was the merriest man alive,
Then, dying at eighty or a bit,
Became a saint by holy wit.

—Phyllis McGinley

In the ancient, medieval, and post-Renaissance world, *comedy* usually included the unexpected triumph of a smaller character or group of characters. In a sense, the comedies were our earliest underdog stories. As the meaning of comedy changed, the word *humor* also emerged, describing the balance of bodily fluids that affect one's well-being. In the sixteenth century the word took on the meaning of one's whim and ability to change mood. Thus, a humorist became one who was witty and brought out joy in others.

In no way does calling Philip Neri a "man of humor" mean that he was a "funny guy." The humorous things that he did were usually not directed to making others laugh. Even though they often did, he was not some kind of comedian-saint. Philip's sanctity did not derive from his sense of humor; rather, the great humor that Philip was known for came *through* his saintly life. His unpredictable demeanor, his random penances and mortifications, and the unpredictable governance of his Congregation of the Oratory, which categorically made him a man of humor, were a product of his personal holiness and ambition to make everyone around him holy. He tells us, "The true way to advance in holy virtues, is to advance in a holy cheerfulness."[121]

At the time of the Counter-Reformation, much of the Christian world was devoid of joy, and the Rome in which Neri would take up his ministry was spiritually bleak. Philip was a total contradiction to his surroundings. He had a clear and deep sense of joy for the gospel and a contagious sense of humor, whether people were laughing at him or with him. This sense of humor can be learned, and can serve every Christian in the discipleship of others and the evangelization of the world at large.

There are two main ways we can learn from St. Philip Neri. First, we can cultivate a love for true joy and share it with the world. Second, through intention and practical methods, we can learn to embrace complete humility even if we look like fools. A wonderful quote popularly attributed to St. Neri:

> We are not saints yet, but we, too, should beware. Uprightness and virtue do have their rewards, in self-respect and in respect from others, and it is easy to find ourselves aiming for the result rather than the cause. Let us aim for joy, rather than respectability. Let us make fools of ourselves from time to time, and thus see ourselves, for a moment, as the all-wise God sees us.

There are many kinds of joy and while it is a fruit of the spirit, not every source of joy is godly.[122]

True Joy

Having a proper understanding of joy is imperative to becoming a saint. Joy is the arousal of some sense of good. When we malign and obscure good, we malign and obscure joy. St. Gregory the Great tells us, for example, that (a false) joy may result from another's misfortune (CCC 2539). The unrighteous presence of envy, in this case, corrupts true joy. There's a better means of obtaining the joy that comes from the Spirit, and a study of the life of Philip Neri reveals this.

A story is always told of his youth in which he came upon a donkey filled with apples headed for his house. He was nine years old, and Philip decided to have a bit of fun at the expense of the delivery of goods paid for by his father and mother. Fearless, he climbed upon the donkey's back for a ride and was quickly thrown to the ground when the ass lost its balance, and the full weight of the animal landed on him. Quickly his parents rushed to the scene expecting a certain death, only to find little Philip unharmed by the grace of God. This protection was a significant event to Philip and though he was reverent of the Lord, he took up a new realization of purpose in his life at the sparing of his life.

Another incident occurred around this time that taught young Philip a great lesson in how he should treat others, and what sort of person he wanted to be known as. His younger sister Catherine, playful as any sibling, thought it would be funny to bind Neri and their other sister Elizabeth with rope. Whatever her intentions were, Neri found an opportunity when his sister was vulnerable to move in and give his sister a good shove. When his father scolded him for it, Philip burst into tears of repentance and regret for what he did.

These two events reveal much about the saint and how he matured from his adolescent "Pippin," as he was called, to a different nickname given to him by none other than St. Ignatius of Loyola: "the Bell." So called because he made a joyful noise that attracted those around him to himself and to his society, the Congregation of the Oratory.

We could pass off those early incidents as typical behavior of a young boy learning his boundaries. That's not inaccurate, but it also doesn't serve our goal of holiness. If Philip's father had not applied the right amount of discipline and counsel to his son, our little saint might have gone on to push the boundaries further and if still unchecked, wind up with life-long vices. Philip needed to learn to ward off temptations disguised as true joy—and so must we.

After his ordination to the priesthood, Philip had become tremendously popular in Rome, which caused some to treat him with disdain and spread gossip about his intentions. They accused him of pride, unholy ambition, and having a vice for attention, and sought to have him removed from all activities he was involved in. Some sent for the attention of the vicar general of Rome, who questioned, then rebuked and threatened Neri with prison, before ordering him to cease all his activities.

How did Neri receive this clear and undeserved abuse? With cheer! He informed his accusers that he was not interested in a popularity contest, but worked each day for the glory of God, and promised to remain obedient to whatever wish his superiors would have for him. Feeling patronized, the vicar general grew even more angered and dismissed Philip from his house.

In private, though, Neri was greatly troubled by these accusations, for what he loved and cherished had been taken from him. Yet he still treated his enemies with kindness until they were overcome with love for him by his mighty and courageous charity. Each of his oppressors regained confidence in Philip with full remorse. Neri was able to resume his activities, attracting even more to his following in Rome.

This is a powerful story of Neri's cheerful humility in action. Where others would have faced their accusers with defensive rebuttals, aiming to correct any wrong, especially when what they were doing was in service of the kingdom of God, he simply replied okey-dokey. But Neri's character is full of irony. His wisdom, told in his own words, smacks of this holy contradiction:

> He who really wishes to become a saint must never defend himself, except is a few rare cases, but always acknowledge himself in fault, even when what is alleged is untrue.[123]

We observe this in the very example of Christ when accused by Pilate:

> And as soon as it was morning the chief priests, with the elders and scribes, and the whole council held a consultation; and they bound Jesus and led him away and delivered him to Pilate. And Pilate asked him, "Are you the king of the Jews?" And he answered him, "You have said so." And the chief priests accused him of many things. And Pilate again asked him, "Have you no answer to make? See how many charges they bring against you." But Jesus made no further answer, so that Pilate wondered (Mark 15:1-5).

Neri understood that truly joyful character is steadfast and unwavering when tested. Even if it is our own Church leaders who question us, perhaps even treat us unjustly, even then we must remain joyful, aware of the devil lurking and attempting to create division. Philip tells us:

> Our enemy, the devil, who fights with us in order to vanquish us, seeks to disunite us in our houses, and to breed quarrels, dislikes, contests and rivalries because while we are fighting with each other, he comes and conquers us and makes us more securely his own.[124]

True joy works together with the other fruits of the spirit, especially faithfulness, patience, and self-control. A true sense of joy is pure as gold, and everyone reacts well to gold which is why, eventually, his accusers praised him for his purity.

There is more from the life and words of Neri that clarifies his true sense of joy and how we can put that to use in serving others.

The day before his death was the Feast of Corpus Christi, and Philip offered Mass in the afternoon after hearing confessions for most of the day. He seemed so fit that day that his friend and physician, Angelo Vittorio, remarked that he could live another ten years (he was seventy-nine). That night, after having retired to his quarters at the normal time, he ate his usual sparing meal and went to rest.

But, as he revealed to Nero, who was one of his closest companions, he had been given supernatural knowledge that he would pass on the Feast of Corpus Christi just as St. Gonzaga, and, desiring no extra attention, wanted to prove to those present that he was in a correct state of mind. So he asked one of those present what time it was. It was three hours after sunset.[125] "Three hours," he replied. "If you add two onto that, it makes five, if you add three, it makes six. Off to bed with you!" Even at nearly eighty, knowing he was living his last night, our saint kept his sense of humor and used it to deflect attention from himself.

People witnessed his humor even immediately after his death, when he appeared to a devout virgin woman in a dream and held a lengthy conversation with her. When the banter became trivial he said to the woman, "Let me continue on my journey, you have delayed me long enough." What's ironic, and true to Philip's sense of humor, is that the woman did not know Philip was deceased until the next day when she told the story to members of his society, but Philip, having died and now being outside time and space made a reference to his tardiness—as if that mattered!

Neri is also said to have appeared after death to another virgin woman of devout faith, and to this woman he offered the means of obtaining true joy:

> As you can see, I am being carried up to heaven to receive the reward of my labors: you must therefore do all you can to persevere until death in the way of life you have undertaken. If you do that, you will come to share in my joy, and you have nothing to fear, for I will pray to the Lord for you continually.[126]

Philip Neri was a man of abiding joy and solemn humor. He cracked funnies when things didn't seem to be so funny. Who makes jokes about the time of night just before dying? Even when others were held in a state of fear and anxiety, his antidote was cheer:

> To a sick priest: "Be of good cheer, you will recover from this present illness."[127]

> To one close to death: "Be of good cheer, you will most certainly not die of this illness."[128]

> To a woman filled with terror: "Be cheerful, you have nothing to fear, believe me."[129]

His words should fill us up with saintly cheer, his stories should make us laugh, and his life should make us contemplate the mysteries of the devout life. In his own words:

> Cheerfulness strengthens the heart and helps us to persevere. The true way to advance in holy virtues, is to advance in a holy cheerfulness. The cheerful are much easier to guide in the spiritual life than the melancholy. A servant of God ought always to be in good spirits. Charity and cheerfulness, or charity and humility, should be our motto.[130]

Fools for Christ

Any avid follower of the life of Philip Neri will be familiar with his chief biographer, Antonio Gallonio, a member the Oratory who became a faithful disciple of the saint. His *Life of St. Philip Neri* is mostly written in the third person but quickly takes on the perspective of an eyewitness, since Gallonio was by Neri's side for the latter part of the saint's life, including the night of his death. Most of the stories included in the biography came from the mouth of Philip himself.

With this level of intimacy in mind, it is interesting that although much of Neri's repute has been associated with humor, the vast majority of the stories Gallonio includes are about his prophetic gifts, his ability to heal, his gift of foresight, and countless other cases of intercession and miracles.

> God adorned Philip with great prudence, which was most noticeable in the things he did for the glory of God, and in giving spiritual advice. In order to conceal this virtue, he pretended to be simple and foolish, to be able to say, like St. Paul, 'We are fools for Christ's sake'. He made it his endeavor in everything he did to hide his outstanding discernment under the guise of simple stupidity.[131]

With no uncertainty, we can detect that Gallonio did not wish for Neri to be remembered by his jokes alone, but by his amazing and unique humility.

Now, "humility" is an interesting word with several senses. It can refer to someone who has chosen a humble way of life, or someone who avoids bragging about himself. Before all Christians there is a choice of which type of humility we wish to obtain: that of mortification or that of ignominy. Neri tells point-blank the difference and which one to choose:

It is very necessary to be cheerful, but we must not on that account give in to a buffooning spirit. Buffoonery incapacitates a person from receiving any additional spirituality from God.[132]

Neri wished for his disciples to become fools, not idiots. Neri's life, and more still, his words, show us the true path of humility that comes from being a fool for Christ, not a buffoon.

Neri was certainly no idiot. He was highly astute and surpassed his peers during his studies in Rome. He excelled in the study of philosophy and therefore in disputations, in which his intellect showed. He digested of the works of St. Thomas Aquinas, and his peers, especially Borromeo, de Sales, and Bellarmine, revered him for his intellect and command of theology and philosophy.

Indeed, most of our Counter-Reformation saints knew each other quite well, and their individual personalities come to life when we see them interacting. One unforgettable story, demonstrating Neri's diplomatic tact, involves Neri, Charles Borromeo, and Robert Bellarmine.

Borromeo was busy with correcting the insatiably corrupt city of Milan. Charles was in great need, at least to him, of an orator to preach against the stifling heresies, and would settle for no less than his own choice of priests. He wrote Philip Neri. Then he began to pester Neri. Philip wrote a lovely note in return:

"You accuse me of not being mortified because I will not let you have Fr. Baronius, but I am certain, and by your leave I am going to tell you so frankly, that you are far more lacking in detachment. Many people, including the bishops of Rimini and Vercelli, say this about you, and also that you are not above downright robbery. When you set eyes on a capable man, you immediately try to allure him to Milan. You are a most daring and audacious robber of holy and learned men. As the proverb said, you despoil one altar in order to adorn another."[133]

He understood how to make his point in a respectful, though direct way.

In the process of becoming a righteous fool, Neri did some hilarious things. The above mentioned Fr. Baronius is Cardinal Caesar Baronius, but before he ever became a cardinal and the eventual successor to Neri, our saint would play some practical jokes on the young priest. One time, Neri sent him shopping for wine, tasking him to taste each one to be sure he chose the correct bottle. When Baronius returned, our saint remarked that he only required half the bottle chosen. A time later, Neri charged Baronius to make a complete history of the Church and when manuscripts were presented to him, Neri shrugged and tossed them over his shoulder. *What torment!* But his companions understood that Neri wanted to accomplish two things at all times: help others not take themselves too seriously, and increase virtue.

As we can see, these actions were mortifications, but less physical than that of traditional mortifications. Neri's were *spiritual* mortifications.

> Outward mortifications are a great help toward the acquisition of interior mortification and other virtues . . . Those who pay a moderate attention to the mortification of their bodies, and direct their main intention to mortify the will and understanding, are more to be esteemed than they who give themselves up exclusively to corporal penances and macerations.[134]

He often applied this advice to real-life circumstances. When a member of the Oratory proposed a mortification involving coarse and itchy hair to be worn as a stress to the body, Neri corrected him, having him wear the hair shirt on the outside instead, as a stress to the temperament. Other stories include him meeting important persons with half his beard shaven, and showing up to public events with a chair cushion secured to his head. Small wonder Neri placed a sign above his door reading, "House of Christian Mirth."

But these stories also tell of great purpose and humility in Neri. Philip shares several proverbs to help us understand and attain this humility:

> One of the best means of obtaining humility, is sincere and frequent confession.[135]

> Beginners should look after their own conversion and be humble, lest they should fancy they had done some great thing, and so should fall into pride.[136]

> Humility is the true guardian of chastity.[137]

Close to his death, while suspended in levitation during a vision of the Blessed Virgin Mary, Neri remarked only a single essential piece of counsel: "Anyone who wants something other than God is a fool! Anyone who loves something other than God is a total wreck."[138]

Being the right kind of fool, God's fool, is the ultimate message from the life of St. Philip Neri. It is good to study, great to perform works of charity, and excellent to seek holiness, but it is all a complete waste of time if it is done for the wrong intention. As we seek to be reformers and leaders within the Church, let us earnestly take to mind the words of our Reformer of Solemn Humor: "They who when they have got a little devotion think they are some great one, are only fit to be laughed at."

Conclusion

Neri was a saint like no other: funny, though solemn; authoritative, though polite; tranquil, though active. His life was one of constant work and leadership. He kept his book of jokes, but he was no jester. He made his appeals with verbal muscle to his colleagues, but he always addressed others with humility and tact. He completed his devotions and work with energy, but he never over-exerted himself. Neri had a patient understanding of the borders of discretion, understanding the biblical meme: "For everything there is a season, and a time for every matter under heaven" (Eccles. 3:1).

What's awesome about Neri is that he never sought out these roles: he constantly denied his own merit in leading others. He was ambitious, but only about the eternal safety of others. After leaving home for Rome, St. Philip Neri never returned. So it must be with us.

Readers eager to find more about Philip Neri should begin with the first and most popular biography of the saint from Antonio Gallonio, *The Life of St. Philip Neri*. His work is a masterpiece, and no one is better suited to detail the events of his life and ministry than someone from his inner circle of friends. Gallonio was among his first followers and vividly details Neri's death, for which he was present. A much shorter but satisfying biography is V.J. Matthews's *Saint Philip Neri*. And although the title and author of the legendary book of jokes Neri always kept near his office is not readily known, there is a book of maxims and sayings available that contains a large number of cited and unsourced quotes generally attributed to the humorous saint.

Prayer to St. Philip Neri

O holy St. Philip Neri, patron saint of joy, you who trusted Scripture's promise that the Lord is always at hand and that we need not have anxiety about anything, in your compassion heal our worries and sorrows and lift the burdens from our hearts. We come to you as one whose heart swells with abundant love for God and all creation. Hear us, we pray, especially in this need (make your request here). Keep us safe through your loving intercession, and may the joy of the Holy Spirit which filled your heart, St. Philip, transform our lives and bring us peace. Amen.

Prayer to Know and Love Jesus
by St. Philip Neri

My Lord Jesus, I want to love you but you cannot trust me. If you do not help me, I will never do any good. I do not know you; I look for you but I do not find you. Come to me, O Lord. If I knew you, I would also know myself. If I have never loved you before, I want to love you truly now. I want to do your will alone; putting no trust in myself, I hope in you, O Lord. Amen.

Chapter 8

St. John of the Cross
The Contemplative Reformer

1542–December 14, 1591
Feast Day: December 14

*"All the beauty of creatures compared
to the infinite beauty of God
is the height of ugliness."*

In the sixteenth century the University of Salamanca was an academic haven, producing some of the best biblical and theological scholars in Spain, some of whose works endure to this day as strong and wonderful as its stone facades. Roaming the columned walkways and stony campus grounds one could find students in variously colored robes, each representing the different college of study. There were the religious students too, donning the black, white, or other colors worn by their order. There, too, was a young man dressed in Carmelite brown, desirous of a proper education and a spiritual tradition to accompany it.

But Juan de Yepes, about twenty-five at the time, had decided to leave the Carmelite life. He was in search of a religious life that was more strenuous. He believed that the time he spent with the Carmelites in Salamanca was worthwhile for his studies, but it also left him without much spiritual development. Juan respected the Carmelite order's primitive rule, which was more stringent, but it had been relaxed in 1432 by Pope Eugenius IV and further moderated since.

He looked to the ascetic life of the Carthusians, and while studying with Carthusians in Santo Matía he was approached by a nun from a nearby Carmelite monastery, who was anxious to find help in reforming her order. She sought out Fr. Juan and the meeting was a success. He promised to stay a Carmelite, so long as her plans did not take too long. She recalled the meeting in her diary:

> The young father's name was Fray Juan of the Cross. I praised our Lord. And when I spoke with this young friar, he pleased me very much. I learned from him how he also wanted to go to the Carthusians. Telling him what I was attempting to do, I begged him to wait until the Lord would give us a monastery and pointed out the great good that would be accomplished if in his desire to improve he were to remain in his own order and that much greater service would be rendered to the Lord. He promised me he would remain as long as he wouldn't have to wait long.[139]

The young friar, the future St. John of the Cross, dedicated himself to these plans and in the end he did not just help reform an order, but reformed himself, and produced the Church's most famous works of contemplative spirituality. His teachings for us are challenging and humbling, not to be read without bearing in mind that, like his desires for his Carmelite order, he desired to uphold the strictest standard of Christian virtue, no matter what it took. (The nun, who played a handy role in the discipleship of Fr. John, was none other than St. Teresa of Ávila.)

A Candle in Darkness

John's passion for reforming the lax Carmelites was so strong that he would spend nine months imprisoned in a monastery jail for it. During this time he went through a trying and purgative spiritual crisis that formed part of the basis for his writings on the "dark night of the soul." Many saints have experienced this deep and dark misery in which they no longer relished spiritual devotions and received no pleasure from prayers and service to God. John's works exploring this experience reveal the demands of the spiritual life, and the real hope and joy that come from an independence from worldly troubles.

In addition to this and other intense literary contributions to spiritual matters and the growth of the soul, he remained stubborn in his desire to reform. But he was not stubborn to the point where he let it affect his ability to work with and respecting the opinions of others, nor did he let his stubbornness make him pigheaded; his was a determination, a resolve to do what he knew was right for the glory and love of God, even if it meant he would be hunted, imprisoned, or despised. We can learn from his tenacity to perform powerful works of mercy, both corporal and spiritual. He was a contemplative, after all—and we can be contemplatives, too.

John of the Cross stands before us as a candle in darkness. Many of us will from time to time experience a darkness of the soul that is more like a slump, the inevitable valleys of life. Others will experience a spiritual darkness that is more like a purgatory in which all spiritual enjoyment vanishes and it's no longer a pleasure to serve God. Both souls must continue on and persevere with whatever cross and burden our Savior lays on us; St. John shows us how to do this successfully.

Mystic Humility

John was a contemplative and had many mystical experiences. But don't let that intimidate you. Although many saints experienced visions, ecstasies, trembling, or other phenomena as a special grace, the same has also happened to those who would not be considered mystics. What is a mystic, anyway? It its purest sense, a mystic is one who takes up a life of contemplative spirituality, and enjoys a heightened sense of supernatural realities. Although they may also devote themselves to active spiritual works like teaching, caring for the sick, or missions, mystics spend much of their time in silent contemplation; rather than an active exterior life, contemplatives focus on the interior life and greater union with God. From time to time, they are the ones who tell us the innermost things of the human experience, spirituality, virtue, and holiness. But their goal is not to be sages; rather it's to align their lives with Christ in an inward intimacy. With that being said, anyone can be a contemplative, but it's not easy.

If you've never read the works of John of the Cross, including *Ascent of Mount Carmel*, *Dark Night of the Soul*, and *The Spiritual Canticle*, put them at the top of your priority reading list immediately. He is a spiritual barometer and a kick in the butt rolled up in a couple of books. He challenges our lukewarmness and laxity. If you weren't uncomfortable with your current spiritual life, you will be.

John splits Christians into two general groups: beginners and advanced. Nearly all of us are in the "beginners" group, and that's okay. It is important for every Catholic to take up, in the attitude and imitation of this Counter-Reformer, a self-diagnosis of spiritual health. For those who want to explore a deeper life in the area of contemplative spirituality, his words are your guide.

John begins to help our interior reflection by examining the seven deadly sins: pride, covetousness, lust, anger, gluttony, envy, and sloth. On the surface, in a sensual sense, we might not be guilty of any of these directly. But John is all about the interior life, the spiritual dimensions of sin, and so a more thoughtful examination of conscience is needed. The first sin is *pride*, which is the primary interior sin that many struggle with. Sensually prideful people *say* prideful things and perform prideful *actions*, but many sin with interior pride of ill intent, corrupted motives, and vain desires. Interior pride comes in numerous forms and can most often be found when people wish to instruct than to be instructed, or want to speak of spiritual things—perhaps finishing others' sentences—rather than remaining quiet in active listening. More severe forms include wishing to condemn others who do not have the same kind of devotion they do, or the devotion they want. Others boast, but only to themselves, feeling sorry for others who do not meet their superficial expectations. A powerful and easy way to sin with spiritual pride is to want to *appear* to be holy, and want to appear holier than others. John says,

> Some of these [beginners] become so evil-minded that they do not want anyone except for themselves to appear holy; and so by both word and deed, they condemn and detract others whenever the occasion arises. If their spiritual directors, confessors, or superiors disapprove of their spirit and method of procedure, they feel that these directors do not understand them, or that their failure to approve derives from [the confessor's] lack of holiness. So they quickly search for some other spiritual adviser more to their liking, someone who will congratulate them and be impressed by their deed.[140]

At first look, something like this might seem extreme. After all, most decent Catholics are not envious of the holiness of others. But then again, in some measure, this tendency does exist in all of us. How many of us surround ourselves with people who dislike us or disagree with our ways? How willing are we to collaborate with people who do not return favor to us? It's something to consider. And there's more. St. John brings this lesson to the confessional and private audiences. "Many want to be the favorites of their confessors, and thus they are consumed by a thousand envies and disquietudes. Embarrassment forbids them from relating their sins clearly, lest their reputation diminish."[141] This includes confessing sins to a priest and, without being colorful, hushing some details that might embarrass, or minimalizing details in order to protect egotism. Have you ever waited in line at the confessional when the priest walked by and hoped not to be noticed, or switched confessors if you were? Or do you take on the full burden of humiliation and make yourself a holy holocaust for the sake of full penance and restitution prior to the gift of reconciliation?

If we're so desperate to protect our reputation, if we seek the praise of others, paradoxically we prove how little we actually value ourselves by valuing words and not the reality of our baptism. Either we put our joy and hope in Christ, or we put our joy and hope in comforts.

The second sin to contemplate is *greed*, often referred to as covetousness or avarice. A vital trait of being unified with Christ is the concept of *spiritual poverty*. Now, some may use this term to mean that a person's spiritual condition is destitute, devoid of the "riches" found in Christ (perhaps based on verses like Philippians 4:9, "And my God will supply every need of yours according to his riches in glory in Christ Jesus"). Or they may use it to mean a lack of reward from God for righteousness (see 2 Cor. 9:10-11). But these interpretations are not reflective of the true spiritual poverty described in the Beatitude: "Blessed are the poor in spirit" (Matt. 5:3). It's a spiritual simplicity that puts the interior life first.

> Many never have enough of hearing counsels, or of learning spiritual maxims, or of keeping them and reading books about them. They spend more time doing this than striving after mortification and the perfection of the interior poverty to which they are obliged. Furthermore, they weigh themselves down with over-decorated images and rosaries. They prefer one cross to another because of its elaborateness.[142]

John makes a helpful clarification for us: "What I condemn is possessiveness of heart and attachment to the number, workmanship, and over-decoration of objects."[143] What is important to developing spiritual poverty is *intent*. We can own massive libraries, but they aren't for show. Our altars or prayer candles can be expensive or inexpensive, but we should be indifferent about the aesthetics and worth of these things. Our intent should be focused on how these items aid our devotion. (John tells of a person he knew that had a rosary made of fish bones who fared better spiritually than any he knew.)

The sin of *lust* is next and it is not just lust for sexual things, but also lust for spiritual things. It is very much like envy. This might strike us as odd, but remember that the soul is the form of the person and the person encompasses both body and flesh. Naturally, we receive pleasure from our sensual *and spiritual* devotions and this can be problematic for souls. Read the words of our spiritual father:

> [Beginners] often proceed from the pleasure human nature finds in spiritual exercises. Since both the spiritual

and the sensory part of the soul receive gratification from that refreshment, each part experiences delight according to its own nature and properties. The spirit, the superior part of the soul, experiences renewal and satisfaction in God, and the sense, the lower part, feels sensory gratification and delight because it is ignorant of how to get anything else, and hence takes whatever is nearest, which is the impure sensory satisfaction . . . Because of this, some souls grow sick in their prayer; others give up entirely, for they think these feelings come while they are engaged in prayer rather than at any other time.[144]

Beginners also have very many imperfections and expressions of *anger*, which is the next sin. John tells us that many get angry even after prayer.

Because of the strong desire of many beginners for spiritual gratification, they usually have many imperfections of anger. For when the delight and satisfaction procured in their spiritual exercises passes, these beginners are naturally left without any spiritual fervor . . . they are so unbearable that nobody can put up with them. This frequently occurs after they have experienced in prayer some recollection pleasant to the senses. After delight and satisfaction is gone, the sensory part of the soul is naturally left vapid and zestless . . . They become angry over the sins of others . . . They become so aware of their own imperfections, that they grow angry with themselves in unhumble impatience.[145]

Satan wants you to dislike prayer by tempting you to become angry, or by tempting you with the sensual gratifications that come from spiritual exercise. Ever been angry after prayer, fought with your spouse on the way home from Mass, or yelled at another driver after leaving confession? This has happened to all of us, right? By relating your spiritual life to anger or tempting you to rely on enjoyment in spiritual exercises, Satan is able to use lust against you. To combat this we must ignore the part of us that *wants* to pray and contemplate, and be content to do these things out of *obligation*. If we get enjoyment, good, but we shouldn't rely on it.

Similar to spiritual lust, there is also a form of spiritual *gluttony* that beginners exhibit. This, John makes clear, is a vice for nearly every Christian: "There are hardly any persons among these beginners, no matter how excellent their conduct, who do not fall into some of the many imperfections of this vice."[146] Spiritual gluttony, like physical gluttony, stems from an incomplete regard for moderation in consumption. Where a glutton who has a love for wine might drink too much and become drunk, opening himself to bad decisions and indiscretion, a spiritual glutton is "lured by the delight and satisfaction procured in their religious practices."

What does this refer to? John says that some "will kill themselves with penances ... weaken themselves by fasts they cannot sustain" and "work without counsel or command of another" that is "contrary to obedience."[147] He is not telling us that it is bad to have mortification or to seek penances or to practice other forms of spiritual devotion, but that some will confuse obligation with appetite. Beginners gain enjoyment and pleasure from merely consuming these spiritual devotions, turning away from one in trade for a new penance, or from one form of prayer to another because they are bored and what they have spiritually eaten has become tasteless to them. The secret to overcoming this, just like lust, is realizing that the true contemplative life is not based on an appetitive spirituality, but on obligatory spirituality.

Christians will quickly advance to overcome spiritual gluttony when they commit to these spiritual acts out of *duty*
rather than *enjoyment*. This is why John's "dark night" is a
place of zero enjoyment for spiritual things: the follower of
Christ is progressing away from doing things for enjoyment
and moving toward doing them from duty. Another form of
spiritual gluttony is what we might call sacramental gluttony:
when we frequently refuse to abstain from the reception of
the Eucharist even though we know perfectly well that we
are not in a state of grace.[148]

Envy and *sloth*, the last of the capital sins, might seem quite
dissimilar but are closely related. Spiritual envy is much like
avarice, but it is a deeper self-seeking disorder. When we are
greedy we want more of what we already have, but when we
are spiritually envious we literally grieve that others have what
we don't. We may get angry at another person because of his
goodness, convincing ourselves he is excessively or inauthenti-
cally holy. As John notes, "learning the virtue of others" can
make us "sad."[149] And what a sadness this is—leading us to sloth
when we don't see our own virtues increasing quick enough.
Again, the way to overcome this is to remember that Satan
deceives us into these spiritual perils, banking on our flesh.

None of us want to be beginners forever, especially if we
want to be true reformers like the heroes of the Counter-
Reformation, so how do we combat the tendencies of spiritual beginners? John would say that we should focus less about
how much and *in what way* we seek spiritual devotions, and
more on *why* we seek them and *in what quality*. For example,
there is no such thing as being a "better prayer" than another;
there is only having a pure intent in one's heart. In spiritual
matters, there is less of a measuring stick for devotion, and
more of an on/off switch for intention. Here's how John puts
it into context for us:

Souls, however, who are advancing in perfection act in an entirely different manner and with an entirely different quality of spirit. They receive great benefit from their humility by which they not only place little importance on their deeds, but also take very little self-satisfaction from them. They think everyone else is far better than themselves, and usually possess a holy envy of them and would like to emulate their service of God.

Since they are truly humble, their growing fervor and the increased number of their good deeds and the gratification they receive from them only cause them to become more aware of their debt to God and the inadequacy of their service to him, and thus the more they do, the less satisfaction they derive from it. Their charity and love makes them want to do so much for God that what they actually do accomplish seems as nothing. This loving solicitude goads them, preoccupies them, and absorbs them to such an extent that they never notice what others do or accomplish ... Moreover, even though others do praise and value their works, these souls are unable to believe them; such praises seem strange to them.[150]

If we want to become contemplatives, to grow into a more intimate relationship with God, we must advance past the spiritual forms of the seven deadly sins, of pride, covetousness, lust, anger, gluttony, envy, and sloth. Humility is the key to all the other virtues. To be complete, anyone gifted with mystical graces should seek the guidance of a spiritual director who would be able to confirm and instruct the spiritual progress of the soul.

There was a moment during his captivity when John was close to thinking he might never escape jail, that he would die in his tiny closet of a cell. His biography says he "was confused and doubted the reasonableness of continuing to resist. He had reached the point where he wished God would let him die. In fact, he prayed for this."[151] His dark night was at its bleakest. An opportunity came one day when the guard who had watched over him for months was assigned elsewhere and he received a new guard. This guard has heard stories about how bad they treated the prisoner and figured it was largely John's fault. But after just a few days his impressions of the prisoner changed dramatically.

His new guard was blindsided by John's sincerity, his willingness to endure such a harsh imprisonment while treating everyone around him better than himself. This is the humility of a contemplative. It's true, John was stubborn in his convictions—especially those that had to do with the reformation of his religious order—but always managed to be even more convicted in humility, and the obligations of religious devotion.

Reform the Status Quo

As we now know, St. John of the Cross did not accept the status quo. But his desire to reform the Carmelite order did not come from an inner arrogance that boosted his own opinions and prerogatives; indeed, he was deeply respectful of the order, its founders, and its leadership, and had concerns only for the integrity and excellence of its founding principles. In order to understand his reform, his life and experiences are worth our examination and application.

When John was a young boy, his father and mother moved their little family to Medina del Campo, in north-central Spain. The place had existed with little significance until, opportunely, the time of Juan's life. Thanks to the growing popularity of trade fairs and the new trade agreement with England, Medina del Campo became a modern city of culture, and with this came the fruits of Catholicism and religious life. Little Juan, about nine years old, did not belong to a family of nobility or any level of wealth, and therefore offered to work a little in order to help support his family. His parents reluctantly agreed, and in these little sessions of work he learned a great deal about the outside world through conversations with craftsmen, traders, and drifters. At the same time, he shined in the classroom—at a school for orphans, the only one his family could afford.

As a teenager he went to work as a nurse at a local hospital, and this experience became a major turning point in his life. Watching the patients suffer was difficult for him, but he saw a new virtue in the lives of those who recovered: virtue that came *from* their suffering. This would become the bedrock of his religious convictions and philosophy.

Soon after he took the position as nurse, being recognized for his spiritual talents he was offered the office of hospital chaplain. As much as the position might have been a natural or logical transition for him, he gracefully declined the offer. During this time the Carmelites had opened a house in Medina del Campo and he decided to be among the first novitiates. John adored the spirituality of the Carmelite order: abstinence, fasting, discipline, austere clothing, all-night vigils, and contemplation.

The order had become somewhat less austere in recent years, though. As one who sought out harsh penances and took very seriously to the idea of silence in religious contemplation, he was the odd man on campus; most of the others viewed him as awkward, too serious, strange, and would often not involve him in meetings and activities. Some admired him, but only to an extent.

In 1567, while studying in Salamanca, he was ordained a priest. Even then he didn't quite fit in. Others would run if he found them talking too loudly, not observing their rule of silence, in fear that he would give them a sermon—which he certainly would. His judgment was not directed to them personally, but toward their willingness to avoid their own rule.

Around this time he was very close to abandoning the Carmelites in order to join the stricter Carthusians. As we saw, though, God—and Teresa of Ávila—intervened, and their energy and ambition would prove to be the recipe for real reform in the Carmelite order, and Spain in general. He aided Teresa of Ávila in forming the *Discalced Carmelites*, named such for their return to the primitive rule that included going barefoot as a form of penance.

The next several years involved much study, planning, administration, and much of his reform work took place prior to the time of his jailing. He and Teresa had already gotten the approval for their reforms, but tensions were growing in the order and others were envious and upset over what they saw as divisiveness. So a group of Carmelites opposed to reform kidnapped him, put him through a speedy and quasi-lawful trial, and jailed him in horrible conditions.

For John and Teresa, reforming an order was as much a legal, political, and administrative process as it was a spiritual one. There is not a formula to be learned from them for reforming each and every problem in the Church today, but there are lessons about the character and virtue required for those who wish to make better of themselves first, and their communities second.

First, a true reformer must be *unattached to worldly things*. John consistently stressed that "individuals must deprive themselves of their appetites for worldly possessions."[152] The issue lies in attachment to these things, wherein we base our happiness on the accumulation of stuff and the hoarding of things that have no eternal value. There is a difference between owning something for utility or proper entertainment and being attached to something for possession's sake. John explains: "It ought to be kept in mind that an attachment to a creature makes a person equal to that creature; the stronger the attachment, the closer is the likeness to the creature and the greater the equality."[153]

Next, reformers should hold strong to the virtue of *hope*. Hope is an absolute necessity if we are to commit our lives to a constant conversion, and it's indispensable as well for those hoping to reform the Church in any measure: be it the culture in their parish, the focus of a small group, the consistency of a local chapter of a third order, or just the domestic church of their own family. John tells us in *The Ascent of Mount Carmel*:

> Our aim is union with God in the memory through hope; the object of hope is something unpossessed; the less other objects are possessed, the more capacity and ability there is to hope for what one hopes for, and consequently the more hope; the greater the possessions, the less capacity and ability for hope; accordingly, in the measure that individuals dispossess the memory of forms and objects, which are not God, they will fix it on God and preserve it empty, in the hope that God will fill it.[154]

Our hope should not be empty or idle. Hope does not involve sitting on a couch waiting for something else to happen: hope involves work and endurance. St. Paul wrote to the Romans,

> Through [Christ] we have obtained access to this grace in which we stand, and we rejoice in our hope of sharing

the glory of God. More than that, we rejoice in our sufferings, knowing that suffering produces endurance, and endurance produces character, and character produces hope, and hope does not disappoint us, because God's love has been poured into our hearts through the Holy Spirit who has been given to us (5:2-7).

We need hope because we're human and will feel tempted at times to give up or to slacken our efforts. Through hope we can resist and focus on what we know to be true, the end state of our work, and the graces that come freely through Christ. In moments we are filled with hope and holy ambitions, John tells us, "As often as distinct ideas, forms, and images occur to them, they should immediately, without resisting them, turn to God with loving affection, in emptiness of everything rememberable."[155]

As we have seen, it is dangerous for our soul to rely on moments of spiritual gratification, because these may be few and far between. Hope allows us to keep our drive even when we're not constantly feeling "fulfilled," and our countenance on them can drive us to lose hope if we are not suddenly "fulfilled." Again, we fall back on the habit of fulfilling our work through *obligation*, rather than pleasure. John says,

> If these things refer to their obligations, they should not think or look on them for a time any longer than is sufficient for the understanding and fulfillment of these obligations. And then they should consider these ideas without becoming attached or seeking gratification in them lest the effects of them remain in the soul.[156]

Understanding the proper concept of *joy* is also important to our work of reform. John calls joy "the first passion of the soul and emotion of the will." He continues:

Joy is nothing else than a satisfaction of the will with an object that is considered fitting and an esteem for it … Active joy which occurs when people understand distinctly and clearly the object of their joy and have the power either to rejoice or not … In this [passive] joy, the will finds itself rejoicing without any clear and distinct understanding of the object of its joy.[157]

Despite his austere religious practices, John was also a very fun person to be around. Once out of prison (after nine months he finally escaped, using a rope made from his bedding), he immediately began giving sermons followed by outrageously funny stories. His joy was based on an understanding that whatever promoted the well-being and growth of the soul—the *satisfaction* as he put it—was considered a good for the person both spiritually and physically. His mystical understanding of this further united him with God by not focusing on one part of the soul over the other, but in appreciation for the growth of the entire human person, body and spirit.

While traveling in Lisbon, he was told about an opportunity to meet a woman who was said to see visions and raptures and had captivated several influential clergy and teachers. John declined, saying: "I did not see the nun, nor did I desire to do so, because I would not think much of my own faith if I thought I would grow one iota by seeing her."[158] John had the highest type of faith without sight. The objects of his joy that enabled him to reform the order were not the junk-food type that last only a short time. (A while later the nun turned out to be a fraud.)

There's much more to be studied about St. John of the Cross's reforming style and accomplishments, but detachment, hope, and joy are the top three we can learn from him.

Christian reform is not about novelties and progress, but is a return to the soul's conversion to Christ. True reform will keep the Church in a constant state of conversion.

Conclusion

St. John of the Cross's impact on the Counter-Reformation required a great deal of suffering and torment. Of course, most saints, in one way or another, endured suffering. Sainthood and true reformation always require self-sacrifice. Even if we never have to endure torture or imprisonment for our faith, all our lives will involve some amount of suffering that God wills to use for our good. We must remain contemplatively humble, avoiding the spiritual sins and cultivating detachment, hope, and joy.

Beginners have the luxuries of spiritual enjoyment, whereas those who are graced to progress further in the spiritual life are eventually going to face the *night*. Our saint's night is an earthly purgatory, which most of us will not endure night while on earth. In any suffering, though, in the low parts of our life, we can be greatly comforted by the witness of John of the Cross.

Avid readers will have fun and be greatly challenged by the writings of St. John of the Cross. *The Dark Night of the Soul* is popular for a number of reasons, and it belongs in the personal library of every Catholic. *The Ascent of Mount Carmel* reads right into *Night* and is also a very satisfying—if dense—read. *The Spiritual Canticle* is poetic and also dense, as is *The Living Flame of Love*, which John wrote in a fortnight. Biographical readers will be thrilled with the layout and pace of *John of the Cross: Man and Mystic* by Richard P. Hardy, which presents his life in an excitingly historical and meaningful context.

Prayer of St. John of the Cross

True to the uniqueness of St. John is the prayer section in this chapter. Rather than provide you with words to pray, John would suggest that you approach God in prayer with few words, listening intently and openly to his still and soft voice. Allow yourself to contemplate and meditate, silently, upon anything he places on your heart. If you have trouble focusing, read a small bit of Scripture or a saint's words and focus on those, returning to those words any time you lose focus.

Chapter 9

St. Jane Frances de Chantal
The Simple Reformer

January 28, 1572–December 13, 1641
Feast Day: August 12

"Hold your eyes on God and leave the doing to him.
That is all the doing you have to worry about."

A middle-aged women with a great marriage, four wonderful children, charged with the custody of an entire estate and its staff is not the sort we would expect to join a convent. Nor is she the sort we'd expect to exchange scores of letters with bishops and cardinals or become a close confidant to a great saint. In Jane Frances de Chantal, at twenty-eight years old, we see a woman who deeply loved God, her children, and her husband, and we wouldn't expect her to do a lot more than live out that simple life in holiness.

But life can be unpredictable, and one day, her husband came home from hunting with a gunshot wound. He died within hours. Her life turned upside down. Overnight she became a single mother with little outside support. Her simple life was not so simple anymore.

But over the rest of her life, having endured some of the worst tragedies to face a mother, she not only raised her children well but founded a religious order and, under the guidance of a man she prophetically said would become a saint, become a saint herself. She did not do all of this with miraculous help, a complex religious life, or a rigorous asceticism. Just because her modest life became complicated did not mean she had to find complex solutions or intricate fashions of devotion to God. She had special grace from God, but her way was a simple way.

Rocky Road to Sainthood

There are many ways to say her name: Jane, Jeanne, Jane Frances, Jane de Chantal, Jane Frances de Chantal, Jeanne-François Frémyot de Chantal, or some combination of these. But it was one and the same Jane born into a prosperous family in Burgundy and who, just eighteen months later, lost her mother. She cultivated rich gifts of spiritual devotion from a young age, but after marrying a baron at twenty-one she had little time, a mountain of responsibilities, and no spiritual direction. Her saving grace, though, came through her defining trait: an undying desire to follow the will of God. This ability to follow God's perfect will can seem convoluted and impossible to many of us. How do we do that, though? St. Jane had much to say on the topic.

> [In] all your good works you should unite yourself to the will of God's good pleasure, and in your faults and imperfections, you should unite yourself to his permissive will gently, quietly, and with peace of mind. [Francis de Sales] used to say: "Let us do all the good we can, faithfully, peacefully, and quietly; and when we are unfaithful, let us make up for this failure by humility, a humility that is faithful.[159]

She discusses this method in a letter to her director, Francis de Sales, bishop of Geneva:

For my part it seems to me that I am in a simple state
of waiting on the good pleasure of God to do whatever
he wills with me. I have no desires, no plans; I hold to
nothing, and very willingly leave myself in his hands;
still, I do this without sensible devotion, but I think it
is all right at the bottom of my heart.[160]

Her entire outlook on her life was complete abandonment
to God's will—letting go to self and letting God take over.
Even down to the way we do things, she instructs that the
best way to be perfect is to just try your best. She told one of
the young novices in France: "You must take care not to fall
into this fault, but be simple; don't think much about yourself
and just do the best you can."[161]

Understanding Jane's life is impossible without frequent
mention and correlation to the life of St. Francis de Sales.
She epitomizes wisdom of studying the saints in order to
become one. Through her correspondence and meetings with
de Sales, through pondering the wisdom in his words and
through obedience to his instruction, she was able to traverse
her rocky road to sainthood. It wasn't pretty and it wasn't perfect—which makes her a perfect saint to study for those of us
who often feel we don't have what it takes to become saints.

Enduring Obedience

We have seen in some of our saints that humble and graceful
opposition to the status quo, even to the hierarchy, can be part
of authentic reform. But Jane's life was marked by a habit of
temporal obedience that translated well into *divine obedience*,
too. Through all her trials and challenges she accepted her
state of life, submitting herself to rightful authorities, faithful to her conviction that God had a bigger plan at work.

Recognizing this enduring obedience, St. Vincent de Paul said of her:

> She was a woman of great faith, and had temptations against the Faith all her life. Even though she appeared to have reached the peace and tranquility of spirit of virtuous souls, she suffered terrible interior trials which she communicated to me on several occasions. She seemed so harassed by abominable temptations that she had to take her eyes away from herself so as not to contemplate her unbearable state. To look at her soul horrified her as if it was an image of hell. But through these great sufferings she never lost her serenity, yielding with joy to what God wanted from her. That is why I consider her as one of the most holy souls I have met on earth.[162]

How do we follow Christ with such obedience and submission? Most of us have heard God's instructions at some point in our life and had trouble saying "yes." If the *Catechism* tells us that "the desire for God is written in the human heart, because man is created by God and for God; and God never ceases to draw man to himself" (27), then how do we become better at following our hearts? Just as water may be purified by passing through filters or boiling, the trials in our lives can be filters that strain out our flaws—or kill them with intense heat.

One of the first ways to achieve this is through *acceptance*. Jane accepted that each step of her life and spiritual journey was equipping her for the next adventure.

There came a special moment early in her life when her grandfather died. She was about fifteen. He had been a servant of the poor, and had inspired her to devote herself to the spiritual life. When he died she resolved to continue his life of service. Around this time, too, she would visit towns and villages where churches and statues had been desecrated by Calvinists and the locals were increasingly hostile to the Catholic faith. This, of course, greatly disturbed her and she could very well have avoided her responsibilities in such places, refused to serve the people there, or become cynical to the life God was leading her on. All of these would have been easy choices, but she chose to accept the situation for what it was, even if it caused her discomfort.

Sometimes, she was stunned by a situation that turned out to be vastly different than she thought it would. She was married to a respectable nobleman, true, but, as her new husband explained, their tenants were not paying rent, the chateau they lived in was only partially complete with little money to pay for the remainder of the work, and his servants habitually stole from them. From early in her marriage she was tasked with bringing the household into order. She was often tempted to worry, but a sage piece of advice she always gave was, "Hold your eyes on God and leave the doing to him. That is all the doing you have to worry about." She returned to this advice often in her life. What would be tempting to view as another impossible challenge was to Jane another opportunity to let Christ's grace work through her, even if she didn't have a clue what would happen next. And what would happen a couple of years later would alter everything.

This event, which any survey of Jane's life cannot omit, is among the ultimate tests of endurance and submission to the will of God that anyone can experience. After bearing four beautiful and healthy children, her happy marriage and perfect future came to a sudden termination when her husband died in a hunting accident. He suffered for several hours before he passed and was able to share some tender and reassuring moments with Jane. But, as any could understand, it took her years to cope and to recover from such a sudden and drastic loss.

During this time she surely must have reflected on our Lord's words in the Gospel of Matthew:

> Therefore I tell you, do not worry about your life, what you will eat or what you will drink, or about your body, what you will wear. Is not life more than food, and the body more than clothing? Look at the birds of the air; they neither sow nor reap nor gather into barns, and yet your heavenly Father feeds them. Are you not of more value than they? And can any of you by worrying add a single hour to your span of life? And why do you worry about clothing? Consider the lilies of the field, how they grow; they neither toil nor spin, yet I tell you, even Solomon in all his glory was not clothed like one of these. But if God so clothes the grass of the field, which is alive today and tomorrow is thrown into the oven, will he not much more clothe you—you of little faith? Therefore do not worry, saying, "What will we eat?" or "What will we drink?" or "What will we wear?" For it is the Gentiles who strive for all these things; and indeed your heavenly Father knows that you need all these things. But strive first for the kingdom of God and his righteousness, and all these things will be given to you as well. "So do not worry about tomorrow, for tomorrow will bring worries of its own. Today's trouble is enough for today (Matt. 6:25-34).

The event was spiritually disorienting and it took a number of years before she was inspired to discern a religious life. Despite the hard reality of her new situation, her unalterable belief in being content with the will of God got her through the transition, and enabled her to redirect her efforts and expectations accordingly. She offered the following advice to another such transitioning soul in 1632:

> All that remains then, as [Francis de Sales] would say, is to humble yourself profoundly under God's hold hand, to let yourself be led in the way of his good pleasure and, following that same good pleasure, to offer no resistance to whatever he may wish to do with you and to correspond to his grace by fidelity to the opportunities presented to you by Providence.[163]

After achieving a state of acceptance of God's will and authority, the next thing to do is to *abandon all desires for advancement*. The apostles had to learn this lesson the hard way. While discussing among themselves their place in heaven and asking Jesus which among them would be the greatest, he shocked them when he said the greatest in the kingdom would be the one who humbled himself like a child (Matt. 18:1-5). Jane provided counsel that agrees with this, and clarified what humility looks like in practice, by explaining that the desire for advancement is a common and certain way to desire a will other than God's. She wrote to a former aristocrat:

> God wants you to temper your overeagerness by calming all this ardor, reducing it to a simple assent of your will to do good quietly—and only because it is God's will. In the same way, yield lovingly to this divine will when it allows you to fail to perform some good deed or to commit some fault. Resign yourself to not being able to resign yourself as completely and utterly as you would like, or as you think our Lord would like.[164]

Abandon all your desires for advancement and perfection; hand them over completely into God's hands.
Leave the care of them to him, and only yearn for as
much perfection as he wishes to give you. I beg you,
toss away all such desires because they will only cause
you to worry and disquiet, and even make it possible
for self-love to creep in imperceptibly. Have only a
pure, simple, peaceful longing to please God, and, as
I have said before, this will lead you to act without
such impetuousness and overeagerness, but with peace
and gentleness. Your chief care ought to be to acquire
this spirit; however, this care must be tender and loving, free of anxiety, even as you wait for results with
unlimited patience and total dependence on the grace
of God. Trust him to bring about these results at the
right time for his glory and your benefit. Do not wish
to possess them any sooner.[165]

Her words are powerful, yet simple. She exhorts us to
give up our personal ambitions for calm and humble expectations of God's will, not our own. Note her insistence that
advancement is not an evil. In God's perfect will, we might
advance, or we might stay right where we are. But always
we must manage our expectations, being silent and content
while God unfolds his plans.

Many of us do have holy ambitions and these must be
separated from unholy intentions and over-eagerness. Even
Jane had to do this. She and Francis de Sales had recruited
some novices for their new Order of the Visitation,[166] and
soon these women were ready to make their solemn professions. Mother de Chantal had no money for veils, so she and
Francis decided to cut some material from the curtains. But
Mother went a step further. In bitter tears she later confessed

to Francis that she had taken money that Francis had given her to feed the poor and used it instead to buy decorations for the altar during the ceremony.

It can be difficult to wait for God to provide something that seems so important to us, especially when we believe it is in service to the Church. It's a crucial lesson to learn, and Jane offers sage advice for those who are willing to be obedient and endure the wait for God's plans: "Simply be ready to carry them out when his divine will presents them to you."[167] When God opens doors, we should walk right through them!

A caveat is necessary, though. Accepting the events and situations in your life doesn't mean you should blindly follow and embrace any change that comes along. Such a test came early in Jane's life when she rejected a marriage proposal from a heretic. Another tough issue came up when she had to make the difficult decision not to accept some women into her order. Despite being docile to God's will, Jane did not accept every single change or scheme that came her way, and we don't have to either. She sought counsel and wisdom from those around her, and when she knew things were not right, she acted. So should we, with prayer and counsel.

Lastly, St. Jane de Chantal teaches us that sometimes, obedience means *accepting our limitations*. We aren't meant to "do it all," and in different stages of our life we will have limits—from younger years when we are still refining our skills and character to later when energy, memory, and strength are not what they once were. We must be obedient to these stages of life. Francis de Sales realized at some point that he could no longer pray for four hours straight because he literally could not hold himself up. Bellarmine lost some memory in old age, often joking that his best years were behind him before his best resources were published. Accepting what we can't or can no longer do is a high mark of spiritual maturity! Our Mother de Chantal says:

> Oh, for the love of God . . . take my word for it, our Lord is more pleased with our accepting the relief our body and spirit require, than by all these apprehensions of not doing enough and wanting to do more. All God wants is our heart. And he is more pleased when we value our uselessness and weaknesses out of love and reverence for his holy will, than when we do violence to ourselves and perform great works of penance. Now, you know that the peak of perfection lies in our wanting to be what God wishes us to be: so, having given you a delicate constitution, he expects you to take care of it and not demand of it what he himself, in his gentleness, does not ask for. Accept this fact. What God, in his goodness, asks of you is not this excessive zeal which has reduced you to your present condition, but a calm, peaceful uselessness, a resting near him with no special attention or action of the understanding will except a few words of love, or of faithful, simple surrender, spoken softly, effortlessly, without the least desire to find consolation or satisfaction in them. If you put that into practice, my dear [friend], in peace and tranquility of mind, I promise you, it will please God more than anything else you might do.[168]

In her lifetime, Jane endured the gamut of ways to be challenged and ways to be hurt, and her loving advice to persist in and rise through each of these is to remain watchful for God's will by abandoning our desires for advancement and accepting—even embracing in holy humility—our uselessness when it comes.

Simple

Sometimes the simpler a thing seems, the more we are fascinated by its power. Water is abundant on the earth and makes up most of our bodies. Yet it is actually a unique and strange molecule. It is simple in that it is composed of two hydrogen atoms and one oxygen, but its two nonbonding pairs of electrons cause water to dissolve many other substances as a universal solvent, make it less dense in the solid form than the liquid (ice floats), and provide a relatively high melting and boiling point. In this way, something so simple can be fascinating!

Even simpler than water is God. About 300 years before Mother de Chantal formed her order, St. Thomas Aquinas argued that God, though an all-powerful, all-knowing, and all-present being, is simple. God is simple because he is not composed of parts. He has no body, does not move or change, and has no potential since he is perfection itself.[169] In the same way water is simple and God is simple, Jane's wisdom and virtue are imbued with simplicity. The prayers she recommended and the guidance she provided were not novelties or elaborate orders: they were practical, easy to understand, and reliable. Her time called for epic heroism in the Church, and she was heroic in her simplicity.

What she learned and transmitted to her friends came mostly from her many conversations with Francis de Sales, so she habitually quotes her spiritual director. Many of her simple ideas came from him, but she refined these in her writings to make for some of the most profound expressions of holiness ever given by a saint. Her counsel on simplicity comprises three lessons: desire for God's will, small affirmation of God's presence, and heartfelt, artless prayer. She also offers simple ways to cope with sin and pain—two things we must all do if we want to be a saint.

The desire for God's perfect will is the fundamental article of her instruction. We addressed some of this in the previous section, but it is worth revisiting here. God's will *is* perfect, and that can seem intimidating for many souls, but in a special way, it's easier that we realize. The basic way we can understand her advice on understanding God's will is to "be still." The Lord says, "Be still, and know that I am God" (Ps. 46:10). "Stop!" he says. "Let me do it." Jane tells one soul in a letter:

> Instead of being preoccupied with weighty thoughts, *just gaze at God and let him do what he wills*—these are the words of [Francis de Sales]—because since our divine Savior is the only object of your love and aspiration, and the sole comfort of your dear, beloved heart, you will find in him all you need. In the beginning, especially, you must put this into practice in all simplicity. This will strengthen you in the higher part of your soul and calm the passions of your heart.[170]

To Mother de Chantal, the easiest way to accomplish God's will is to be simple: let God act and don't force things to happen. When we force things to happen it can be catastrophic. We can deceive ourselves into believing that all the plans that backfired are God's fault, when really, we forced *our* plans first. But the more we put in God's hands, the more our yoke lightens (Matt. 11:30).

To the daughters of her order and to anyone who corresponded with her, Jane also commonly recommended *simple acts of affirmation*. Jane's brother, an archbishop, frequently called on her for direction on matters of faith. Despite his office, he struggled with a devotional faith. Luckily, his sister was St. Jane de Chantal. She writes him in 1625:

During the activities of the day, spiritual as well as temporal, as often as you can, my dear [friend], unite your will to God's by confirming your morning resolution. Do this either by a simple, loving glance at God, or by a few words spoken quietly and cast into his heart, by assenting words like: "Yes, Lord, I want to do this action because you want it," or simply, "Yes, Father," or, "O Holy Will, live and rule in me," or other words that the Holy Spirit will suggest to you. You may also make a simple sign of the cross over you heart, or kiss the cross you are wearing. All this will show that above everything, you want to do the holy will of God and seek nothing by his glory in all that you do.[171]

The advice is simple, but fascinating. A mere act like the sign of the cross invokes numerous affirmations of faith: prayer, the Trinity, the Passion, the Incarnation, sanctifying our day, raising up God's name, reaffirming baptism, and more. The simplicity of these affirmations can go a long way in carrying us through our complex lives. The proverb says, "In all your ways acknowledge him" (Prov. 3:4), which is precisely what we must strive to do. Victories for Christ are fantastic as they are advancements of the kingdom, but we must also advance the kingdom of God in our hearts, minds, and souls. Every morning we should rise and make one of these simple affirmations, acknowledging him and giving him our whole selves. Then, at the end of our day, we should similarly dedicate any successes to him and confess anything we did or did not do. In this simple way, we acknowledge God every day and begin to desire his presence and will more and more.

These words of affirmation are paramount to our daily activity, and along with this we also require more focused prayer: time set aside to talk to God about our day, our worries, and our hopes. Mother de Chantal was a religious woman with a structured lifestyle according to the rule of St. Augustine, but with simplicity laced throughout it.

Jane further recommended that non-liturgical prayer should be *prayers from the heart in our own words*. She again instructs the heart and mind of her brother, the archbishop:

> Follow your own way of speaking to our Lord sincerely, lovingly, confidently, and simply, as your heart dictates. Sometimes be content to stay ever so short a while in his divine presence, faithfully, and humbly, like a child before his father, waiting to be told what to do, totally dependent on the paternal will in which he has placed all his love and truth. You may, if you wish, say a few words on this subject, but very quietly: "You are my Father and my God from whom I expect all my happiness." A few moments later (for you must always wait a little to hear what God will say to your heart): "I am your child, all yours; good children think only of pleasing their father; I don't want to have any worries and I leave in your care everything that concerns me, for you love me, my God. Father, you are my good. My soul rests and trusts in your love and eternal providence."[172]

Her main objective was to communicate a prayer life located in the heart of the believer, to talk to God with honesty and simplicity. God doesn't demand that we are poets in prayer. When we adopt her advice we rid ourselves of the burdens of trying to tell God the prettiest and most thoughtful things, making our prayer honest and authentic. Heartfelt prayer frees us to be completely centered and focused on God's presence as often as we can:

Souls drawn to the prayer of simplicity should be most careful to curtail a certain eagerness that creates a desire to be active during the time of our prayer. It is pure self-love that breeds this hankering, and it deprives us of simple attention and occupation to the presence of God.[173]

Nearly all of Jane's letters of spiritual advice mention desire for God's will, simple words of affirmation, and heartfelt prayer. We also find her commonly discussing the problems of *sin* and *pain*.

Her instruction on dealing with sin is, unsurprisingly, *simple*: immediately seclude yourself and make an honest act of confession and contrition to the Lord.

When you have committed some fault, go to God humbly, saying to him, "I have sinned, my God, and I am sorry." Then, with loving confidence, add: "Father, pour the oil of your bountiful mercy on my wounds, for you are my only hope, heal me." A little later: "By the help of your grace, I shall be more on my guard and will bless you eternally," and speak like this according to the different movements and feelings of your soul. Sometimes put yourself very simply before God, certain of his presence everywhere, and without any effort, whisper very softly to his sacred heart whatever your own heart prompts you to say.[174]

Again, our saint urges us to commit to saying heartfelt words, even in confession. Of course along with this, we must take up a full examination of conscience, regularly, in order to prepare ourselves for the sacrament of reconciliation.

Pain comes in a variety of forms, the most serious of which should always be evaluated and/or treated by clinical professionals. But there are many pains in our life that are common to the consequences of the fall and original sin. Pain can act like an infection to the mind, causing us to experience fear and despair. Mother de Chantal offered these words of assistance:

> When you are experiencing some physical pain or a sorrowful heart, try to endure it before God, recalling as much as you can that he is watching you at this time of affliction, especially in physical illness when very often the heart is weary and unable to pray. Don't force yourself to pray, for a simple adherence to God's will, expressed from time to time, is enough. Moreover, suffering born in the will quietly and patiently is a continual, very powerful prayer before God, regardless of the complaints and anxieties that come from the inferior part of the soul.[175]

Jane's counsel on dealing with pain is of a piece with her emphasis on obedience to God's will and on a humble simplicity of soul:

> Suffering is the crucible in which our Lord wishes entirely to purify you. Your interior correspondence ought wholly to consist in a simple handing over of yourself, in a complete self-surrender; then for the exterior, humility, submissiveness and meekness.[176]

Jesus experienced every pain and every temptation associated with it, and he knows and understands our hearts to such perfection that we should feel his presence in every enduring moment.

For sanctity, Jane never recommended anything bold, heroic, or especially rigorous. All we need to do, she says, is surrender to God what is God's, pray from the heart by telling God that we want his will for our lives every single day, and remind ourselves of this through little quiet words.

Conclusion

Among the saints of the Counter-Reformation, St. Jane de Chantal stands out as the one most of us can identify with. So many of us endure hardships with children, marriage, vocation, and other life experiences. She was not the one who rebuked heretics or wrote treatises defending the Faith; her contribution to the Counter-Reformation was a subtle form of asceticism, a simple way to observe the obedience of faith that every Catholic can embrace through triumph and tragedy. She is the Simple Reformer, her entire religious philosophy summed up in this: "Simplicity toward God consists in seeking him only in all our actions."

Saint Jane is a fine example of simplicity in spirituality, and her writings reflect this. They are filled with countless proverbs, pithy, practical, and useful to every soul. To her brother, when he was enduring the hardest trials of his life, she wrote: "An ounce of virtue practiced in time of tribulation is worth more than a hundred thousand pounds exercised in prosperity." Her works are readily available in *Letters of Spiritual Direction*, a volume which includes the dialogue between her and Francis de Sales, and also several letters written to her fellow nuns, princes, bishops, and laymen. This volume is a must-have. For biographies, get *The Life of St. Jane Frances Frémyot de Chantal* by Emily Bowles. "Selected Letters of Saint Jane Frances de Chantal" is another mass of letters that is widely available.

Prayer of St. Jane Frances de Chantal

O most holy will of God, I give you infinite thanks for the mercy with which you have surrounded me; with all my strength and love, I adore you from the depths of my soul and unite my will to yours now and forever, especially in all that I shall do and all that you will be pleased to send me this day, consecrating to your glory my soul, my mind, my body, all my thoughts, words, and actions, and my whole being. I beg you, with all the humility of my heart, accomplish in me your eternal designs, and do not allow me to present any obstacle to this. Your eyes, which can see the most intimate recesses of my heart, know the intensity of my desire to live out your holy will, but they can also see my weakness and limitations. That is why, prostrate before your infinite mercy, I implore you, my savior, through the gentleness and justice of this same will of yours, to grant me the grace of accomplishing it perfectly, so that, consumed in the fire of your love, I may be an acceptable holocaust which, with the glorious Virgin and all the saints, will praise and bless you forever. Amen.[177]

Novena to St. Jane Frances de Chantal

O glorious saint, blessed Jane Frances,
by fervent prayer, attention to the Divine Presence,
and purity of intention,
you attained on earth an intimate union with God.
Be now our advocate, our mother,
our guide in the path of virtue and perfection.
Plead our cause near Jesus, Mary and Joseph,
to whom you were so tenderly devoted, and whose holy
virtues you so closely imitated.
Obtain for us, O amiable and compassionate Saint,
the virtues you deem most necessary for us;

an ardent love of Jesus in the most holy Sacrament,
a tender and filial confidence in his Blessed Mother,
and like you, a constant remembrance
of his sacred passion and death.
Obtain also, we pray, that our particular intention in this
novena may be granted.

V. Pray for us, O holy St. Jane Frances,

R. That we may be made worthy of the promises of
   Christ.

Let us pray: O almighty and merciful God, who granted
to blessed St. Jane Frances, so inflamed with love of you, a
wonderful degree of fortitude through all the paths of life,
and through her, were pleased to adorn your church with a
new religious Order, grant by her merits and prayers that we,
who sensible of our weakness confide in your strength, may
overcome all adversity with the help of your heavenly grace,
through Christ Our Lord. Amen.

Chapter 10

St. Charles Borromeo
Our Consummate Pastor

October 2, 1538—November 3, 1584
Feast Day: November 4

"I admit that we are all weak,
but if we want help, the Lord God
has given us the means to find it easily."

The Shroud of Turin is the world's most famous relic. This cloth, believed to have wrapped the crucified body of Christ, is also perhaps one of the most well-preserved articles of antiquity. In 1578, after surviving the plague that nearly wiped out his city, and having a particular devotion to the Passion of our Lord, the archbishop of Milan took up a pilgrimage to meditate before the cloth that bound God's body. But this is no ordinary pilgrimage story; it is a story that depicts the consummate pastoral quality of St. Charles Borromeo.

In the mid-sixteenth century, the Shroud resided in the city of Chambéry in the French Alps, under the protection of the dukes of Savoy. (The mountain passes added a not-inappropriate element of hardship and danger to pilgrimages there.) When the deadly pestilence had been driven from the region, Charles set out in October of 1578 on a pilgrimage of thanks. But Duke Emmanuel Philibert caught news of the imminent visit and, being an admirer of the future saint, had the cloth transferred under close guard to the city of Turin on the opposite side of the Alps, reducing the cardinal's journey by half. And the duke was not going to pass up the opportunity to make a pilgrimage of his own, so he accompanied the Shroud in order to warmly greet the saint with his own hands and words.

Four days later, with a salvo of artillery and a public convoy, the duke and his sons greeted the cardinal about a quarter-mile from the city walls. In contrast to the pomp, the cardinal was dressed in a poor pilgrim's outfit. The duke had reposed the relic at the Baroque church of St. Lawrence, so Borromeo proceeded there for several hours of prayer and meditation. He did the same at dawn the next day. So that his pilgrimage was not one of solitary worship, he arranged for the next three days to be filled with spiritual exercises, public adoration, and numerous Masses available to all.

On the final day, Charles Borromeo shared in an open ceremony wherein the relic was raised three times solemnly for the people to behold. The air was filled with cries of contrition, and the cardinal, hearing this, decided that an extended encore was in order. Instead of retiring the cloth to its safe location, he displayed it for adoration for the next forty hours. Other local relics were brought to the church to be reverenced and have the stories of their respective saints told to the people in attendance. After a few days, prior to his departure, Borromeo met privately with the duke and his sons. We don't know exactly what they discussed, but we do know that the Shroud never went back to Chambéry. It remained in Turin, and that city has been part of its name ever since.

This event is but one of many that demonstrate our saint's marvelous pastoral skills, his shrewd decision making, and his resolve to inspire all souls in his care. His influence on the Counter-Reformation, and on the Church for years afterward, is incalculable. He was composer and conductor in one, orchestrating a harmonious rhythm that would shape the entire movement, one section at a time. His work reformed seminaries, colleges, the priesthood itself, conclaves, religious orders, the selection of cardinals and where they would be appointed, and also included the great task of completing the Council of Trent and carrying out its reforms and decrees. All the while, he strove to make Catholic life rich in joy, contrition, action, and personal holiness.

Saint Charles Borromeo is the *consummate pastor*, exemplifying the qualities of a shepherd given by Peter and Paul in Scripture:

> Titus 1:7-8: "For a bishop, as God's steward, must be blameless; he must not be arrogant or quick-tempered or a drunkard or violent or greedy for gain, but hospitable, a lover of goodness, master of himself, upright, holy, and self-controlled."

> 1 Timothy 3:7: "[He] must be well thought of by outsiders, or he may fall into reproach and the snare of the devil."

> 1 Peter 5:2-3: "Tend the flock of God that is your charge, not by constraint but willingly, not for shameful gain but eagerly, not as domineering over those in your charge but being examples to the flock."

In this chapter we will uncover Borromeo's pastoral qualities by examining his life and writings, and also look at a particular topic that, as we have seen, was close to his heart: the veneration of relics.

Pastoral Care

We don't always have leaders we can trust. And we all know excellent managers who are uninspiring leaders, or exceptional leaders who are dismal managers. The paradigm is common in the world, but pastors of the Church should be *un*common. They must be trustworthy, effective managers, and skilled leaders. This high bar also applies to lay Catholic leaders in the apostolate, as well as to the spiritual leadership we exercise in our families. Let's look at some of the qualities that Scripture mandates for such leaders and how Charles Borromeo models them for us.

Blameless

When Paul tells Titus a bishop must be *blameless*, everything after that is a clarification of how Paul defines the character of a blameless person. He "must not be arrogant or quick-tempered or a drunkard or violent or greedy for gain," and so on. Being blameless, then, is actually different from never doing anything wrong. Being blameless is about doing the *right things the right way*. We can go to Mass every Sunday, but if we go drunk we are certainly not blameless! We can visit the sick, but if we boast about it, we are not blameless.

Numerous things can contribute to our becoming blameless saints, but Paul focuses on avoiding arrogance, a quick temper, drunkenness, violence, and greed. In order to extinguish such things from our life Borromeo offers two remedies: joy for Christ, and silence.

When we are delighted to live our lives for God, it is noticeable. Joy in the gospel means that we are taking up Christ himself as our ambition in life, and that we want to share that with the world:

If a tiny spark of God's love already burns within you, do not expose it to the wind, for it may get blown out . . . This is the way we can easily overcome the countless difficulties we have to face day after day, which, after all, are part of our work. In meditation we find the strength to bring Christ to birth in ourselves and in other men.[178]

Being a follower of Christ and having a personal relationship with him is great, but that relationship is not meant to be kept in a bottle or under a cover: it's meant to be shared with the world. Part of our being "blameless," then, is sharing the love of Christ with everyone around us. And as we do that, of course, we must be careful of what we say. From Genesis to Revelation there are more than 150 references to the tongue, many of which[179] tell us that if we can't guard it, it's better to not use it at all.

The more we say, the more that can be held against us, and without careful thought and consideration a slight slip of the tongue can be an occasion for sin, or to cause another to sin. With the intention of avoiding this, in his vast wisdom St. Charles tells us:

Stay quiet with God. Do not spend your time in useless chatter. . . We must meditate before, during and after everything we do. The prophet says: "I will pray, and then I will understand." This is the way we can easily overcome the countless difficulties we have to face day after day, which, after all, are part of our work. In meditation we find the strength to bring Christ to birth in ourselves and in other men.

Avoiding blame, many times, is as simple as staying silent and learning when to say the right thing at the right time.

Leaders have a heightened responsibility in this: if a leader says something is okay, their people are going to act on it. Likewise, a leader can lead people to error for not speaking when it's necessary to.

Examples to the flock

As important as using our tongues to say the right things is having the integrity to practice what we preach. No one wants to be led by a hypocrite. Nothing will harm the authority of a steward of souls more than telling people to do one thing, then doing the exact opposite. Spiritual leaders must lead by *example*. Charles Borromeo is popularly quoted to share in the wisdom of Paul: "Be sure that you first preach by the way you live. If you do not, people will notice that you say one thing, but live otherwise, and your words will bring only cynical laughter and a derisive shake of the head."[180]

Hospitable, lover of goodness, self-controlled

This is similar to Paul's advice to the Philippians: "Finally, brethren, whatever is true, whatever is honorable, whatever is just, whatever is pure, whatever is lovely, whatever is gracious, if there is any excellence, if there is anything worthy of praise, think about these things." (4:8). Our tradition holds that Titus was not merely a convert and missionary but the bishop of Crete, ordained by Paul himself, so this counsel is to be read in that context.

Our saint upheld these pastoral statutes with the utmost integrity. He was certainly hospitable. During the plague that belted his diocese in 1576, a season of fear, anxiety, death, and mourning, Borromeo did not forsake his city or his duties, though many of his advisers and counselors warned him to do so (thinking him more useful alive than dead). Quoting saints and reading aloud homilies of bishops urging shepherds to remain with their flocks during any storm, he remained in Milan with his people. Indeed, he believed that the pestilence besieging his people was not only a matter of disease and hygiene, but also a spiritual state. He told his advisers and companions:

> Have you fully realized the depth of wretchedness of these poor people, not plague-stricken alone, but forsaken of men, and what is far more deplorable, destitute of spiritual succor, not a single priest being found to take compassion upon them? It is I who am the cause in not having been the first to set the example of aiding them. Still, if God does not send them help in other ways, I know my duty.[181]

He resolved, then, to command spiritual exercises in addition to the practical steps taken to combat the plague. In this he combined his pastoral hospitality with the threefold secret of self-control and holiness: prayer, fasting, and mortifications. Not only did he oversee and guide his people through these spiritual exercises, he performed them himself in place of his people, taking their sins and temporal punishments upon himself.

In addition to this, Borromeo took the time to visit the people of his city, one by one, no matter the risk to his life. He also visited people in nearby villages also suffering from the plague. For those in the city, he reconditioned a section of the cathedral to serve as a hospital. He had his own clothing and linens, and those of donors, sent to the hospital for use by the sick and dying. The bishop was truly leading by example, so when more priests were needed for these works of mercy, he wrote:

Reverend fathers,
I have no need to describe to you the miserable state of
this city, since it is open to the eyes of all, nor to rouse
your compassion, for no one can be so hard-hearted as
to not feel for the afflicted. Yet this I will say, that it is
no ordinary calamity which we have now to endure.
We see men in the hour of their need deprived of the
presence and support of those nearest and dearest to
them. We see them torn from their abodes and dragged
to a place of suffering, which is more like a stable than
a hospital and this with little or no hope of again be-
holding their relatives or homes.

    This would be grievous indeed even if it only con-
cerned the frail bodies which must one day perish,
though there would then be this consolation, that
they would soon be rewarded for their pains by an
eternity of joy. But here it is worse than this: it is not
their bodies alone which are in danger of perishing,
it is their souls, for which I plead. Though reduced
to a condition so desperate, they have none to min-
ister to their needs in spiritual things. Shall we not
be heartless indeed if we stand by and stretch out no
hands to help? Shall we see our brethren and fellow
citizens, our friends and relatives, not only deprived
of comforts in their sufferings, not only tortured with
pain and the apprehension of a terrible death: but shall
we stand idly by and see them without any of the
consolations of religion, which they call on us with
tears to take pity on them, while their very looks tell
us, when they have lost their voices, that their days
are without help and their end almost without hope?
O reverend fathers, here is your opportunity to prove
your title to the name of religious, to effect all your

good desires and resolutions, to serve God by acts of heroic perfection.

I call upon you one and all therefore to devote yourselves generously to this work worthy of your high calling, and to make you service a special obligation to Almighty God, who has vouchsafed to charge himself with the reward of all you do for him. Moreover, I ask it of you as a favor personal to myself, of which I shall never be unmindful.[182]

We might not see the likes of a plague in our lifetime, but we are sure to see in ourselves and in our cities a pestilence of evil. When we do we can practice the remedy of Christian perfection: prayer, fasting, and mortification.

Well thought of by outsiders

Who are the "outsiders" Paul is referring to in 1 Timothy 3:7? The Greek word Paul uses is *éxōthen*, which means "from without," and all lexicons agree that Paul means those who are outside the *Church*. So, Paul is telling Timothy that Church leaders should put a good face forward to the world. This piece of wisdom is especially important today, when the world is so liable to be hostile, and when instant communication leaves nothing hidden. It's paramount to respect how our reputation may impact the Church, and the souls that we wish to draw to it.

Of course, this doesn't mean that we should curry favor with the world by compromising the Faith. And there is certainly a place for righteous disregard for those who oppose the truth. For example, we should not quit attempting to save the unborn from abortion just because a sector of the culture tells us we're "anti-woman" because of it. No, we should never succumb to such "outsider" influence! However, for the sake of our Christian witness we should strive to be well-regarded by unbelievers.

Charles knew this, which is why he went to extra lengths not only to promote his own holiness and that of others, but to secure for the Church a positive public image. Even those who do not accept our faith should never doubt our virtue or our works of mercy and love. These may, by God's grace, someday be instrumental in their conversion.

A writer once said of Borromeo:

> So great was the patience and sweetness of Charles amid various and complicated affairs, that he was never known to utter an ungracious or disdainful word, even to anyone of his household. He gave audience to all who came with unwearied kindness. No amount of fatigue ever prevented him from attending to correspondence, or dictating to others as occasion required.[183]

We should live in a way that makes others to say this about us.

Public Demonstrations of Our Faith

We have already seen the story of Borromeo and the Shroud of Turin. But that was not the only time our saint acted to build up public devotion.

The year before, during Lent of 1577, the people of Milan were in desperate need of increased faith and unity. The city had undergone a torrent of misfortune in prior years and the population had just begun to recover from the plague that had decimated it. Amid fresh anxieties, morale and faith were sliding quickly. Corrupt workers charged with disposing of the clothes and belongings of the afflicted were stealing them instead. There were fears that a new outbreak could result from this, and from the arrival of pilgrims seeking the indulgence of visiting the city's holy sites during Lent. Civil penalties were ignored and not enforced, so Cardinal Borromeo stepped in. He admonished the thieves with the threat of excommunication. Next, he created a special opportunity for the citizens to prepare themselves for Lent and for any criminals to repent for and amend their sins by completely removing the quarantines and opening every holy location as a place to receive absolution. This special endeavor was received with gratitude from all the residents—and it seemed to please God, too, as no new outbreak occurred despite the throngs.

St. Charles had a special love for the veneration of relics. He also understood their immense power; that, like all sacramentals, they combine the spiritual and material worlds in objects through which God can provide special grace. As with all generations, probably, many souls under his care doubted the nature of the spiritual world while attaching themselves to physical pleasure.

Such, indeed, was the popular reality that all the Counter-Reformers were up against. A little more than 200 miles from Borromeo's archdiocese was Geneva, where John Calvin had been brewing novel heresies. By 1578, when Borromeo displayed the Shroud, the region surrounding Geneva was more than three decades into Calvin's errors. And of course, Calvin was not short on words to criticize the holy sheet that rested in Chambery only sixty miles from where his innovations to the Christians were introduced.

How is it possible that those sacred historians, who carefully related all the miracles that took place at Christ's death, should have omitted to mention one so

remarkable as the likeness of the body of our Lord remaining on its wrapping sheet? This fact undoubtedly
deserved to be recorded. St. John, in his Gospel, relates
even how St. Peter, having entered the sepulcher, saw
the linen clothes lying on one side, and the napkin that
was about his head on the other; but he does not say
that there was a miraculous impression of our Lord's
figure upon these clothes, and it is not to be imagined
that he would have omitted to mention such a work
of God if there had been anything of this kind. . . . I
shall conclude with a convincing proof of the audacity
of the Papists. Wherever the holy sudary is exhibited,
they show a large sheet with the full-length likeness of
a human body on it. In short, either St. John is a liar,
or all those who boast of possessing the holy sudary
are convicted of falsehood and deceit.[184]

Whether by proximity or by popularity, Calvin's ideas
were impacting the views of nominal and under-evangelized
Catholics, and Borromeo saw how this created a regression of
faith. But he also knew what the cure was: show the people
these relics and sacramentals and permit them to experience
their character and powers firsthand. This is exactly what
he did in 1577 when he made a solemn procession of the
Holy Nail of the Passion from Milan's Church of the Holy
Sepulcher, so called because it was built with stones from
Jerusalem, where the original church of that name was built
over the traditional site of the Crucifixion.

With resolve to unite the people of Milan and promote
Christian charity and humility, Charles worked with the
governor to allow a Lenten procession of the Holy Nail to
commence in thanksgiving and penance, proper to Lent. He
led the procession himself, raising high the relic in a crystal

enclosure for all in the city to see. The governor, officials, and townspeople followed the procession from one end of the city's walls to the other, rounding back to the cathedral where the nail was displayed for veneration for forty hours. All in attendance were given a replica of the nail as a token of solemn remembrance of the Passion.

Just as in Borromeo's time, today relics contain the power to arouse more-ardent faith and convert even the dullest of souls. Their power is real, and it is biblical. In 2 Kings we read a famous story of the power of a holy man's bones:

> So Elisha died, and they buried him. Now bands of Moabites used to invade the land in the spring of the year. And as a man was being buried, lo, a marauding band was seen and the man was cast into the grave of Elisha; and as soon as the man touched the bones of Elisha, he revived, and stood on his feet (13:20-21).

Biblical references to miracles and inspiration through the touch or proximity of holy relics are not limited to the Old Testament:

> And more than ever believers were added to the Lord, multitudes both of men and women, so that they even carried out the sick into the streets, and laid them on beds and pallets, that as Peter came by at least his shadow might fall on some of them. The people also gathered from the towns around Jerusalem, bringing the sick and those afflicted with unclean spirits, and they were all healed (Acts 5:14-16).

> And God did extraordinary miracles by the hands of Paul, so that handkerchiefs or aprons were carried away from his body to the sick, and diseases left them and the evil spirits came out of them (Acts 19:11-12).

From the infancy of the Faith, Christians have venerated the bones and relics of holy persons in the Church. Polycarp, bishop of Smyrna, also disciple and friend of John the Evangelist, said:

> We took up his bones, which are more valuable than precious stones and finer than refined gold, and laid them in a suitable place, where the Lord will permit us to gather ourselves together, as we are able, in gladness and joy and to celebrate the birthday of his martyrdom.[185]

These opportunities to display and venerate relics are not lost to antiquity. We can not only venerate relics today, we can venerate the *very same relics* that Charles Borromeo and his flock prayed before. In a solidarity that transcends time, we have access to the same Shroud, the same bones and objects, that our past brothers and sisters in the Faith reverenced and through which they received particular graces. The veneration of these relics should not be limited to selective viewings and itinerant exhibitions. We should take a page from the wisdom of Borromeo and avail ourselves of the opportunity to venerate relics, as well as encourage pastors and bishops to display them publicly often.

Did you know that every parish (if it has a fixed altar) has a relic? This is an extraordinary gift to us. Any time we approach an altar we are mere inches from the relics of saints as an opportunity for their powerful intercession. Your diocese also likely has a collection of relics, whether First Class (bones, flesh, hair of saints, or objects from the Passion), second class (an item, such as clothing, book, or a ring, that was touched by a saint), or third class (items that have come in contact with a first- or second-class relic).

What is the right way to use relics? The topic of saint veneration was controversial during the time of the

Counter-Reformation, so we need to be clear why we esteem these saintly antiques. First, it must be clarified that Catholics do not worship and do not pray to relics. Worship is to God, and prayer is made to persons. Instead, these holy antiques are *venerable*.[186] St. Thomas Aquinas quotes St. Augustine:

> If a father's coat or ring, or anything else of that kind, is so much more cherished by his children, as love for one's parents is greater, in no way are the bodies themselves to be despised, which are much more intimately and closely united to us than any garment; for they belong to man's very nature.[187]

Aquinas goes on to clarify:

> It is clear from this that he who has a certain affection for anyone, venerates whatever of his is left after his death, not only his body and the parts thereof, but even external things, such as his clothes, and suchlike. Now it is manifest that we should show honor to the saints of God, as being members of Christ, the children and friends of God, and our intercessors. Wherefore in memory of them we ought to honor any relics of theirs in a fitting manner: principally their bodies, which were temples, and organs of the Holy Ghost dwelling and operating in them, and are destined to be likened to the Body of Christ by the glory of the Resurrection. Hence God himself fittingly honors such relics by working miracles at their presence.[188]

Of course, the Church does not guarantee that the presence or touch of a relics of any class will *guarantee* a miracle or other phenomenon. Relics are not magical amulets; neither the Shroud nor the bones of St. Charles Borromeo contain power within themselves. As Thomas carefully elucidates, the Church teaches that relics may be used as an occasion for God to perform miracles.

With Borromeo as our model, the right way to use a relic is to first of all be inspired, and second, to pray with increased hope and faith, and when continuing in their presence, to live with love and devotion in the spirit of that relic. Pastors and bishops must increase efforts to imitate this example. How glorious would it be to see a relic powerfully exposed in a massive procession through the streets of our cities?

Our saint's timing for displaying relics was not random but intentional and considered. When he revealed a relic, he did so either to coincide with a liturgical season (as Lent in these two examples) or on a saint's feast day. Venerating a saint on his feast day is an occasion for an indulgence, so it was like double merit for the souls taking part of the liturgy and prayers.

There is another item that we must clarify, about a matter that could create scandal without proper regulation. The value of relics is incalculable because they are like the materialization of our faith, and so we follow in the sentiment of St. Jose Sanchez del Rio who said before his martyrdom, "My faith is not for sale." Neither are relics, which canon law (1190) says it is "absolutely forbidden" to sell.

But although we must never buy or sell relics, the occasions on which they are revealed and exposed should inspire us to give alms generously. St. Charles is said to have underwritten these pilgrimages and public events himself, donating the funding for everything down to the replicas of the Holy Nail. as in the story of his procession of the Nail of Our Lord's Passion, he donated the funding necessary to have replicas made and given to all attendees of the final events consummating the procession. He encourages us with challenging words: "Do you believe the location where the

Body and Blood of Jesus Christ resides is worth spending money upon?"[189]

Conclusion

St. Charles Borromeo's life and work were essential to the success of the Counter-Reformation and carrying out the decrees of the Council of Trent.[190] He had the energy, skill, and faith, as well as a talent for knowing all the moving pieces and placing people where they could be best used. As with all the other Counter-Reformers, even if we never achieve his brilliance we can model his character. Few of us will become bishops and fewer still will be tasked to complete an ecumenical council and execute its ordinances! All of us, though, are capable of guiding souls as pastors, leaders in the apostolate, and witnesses to our families. Also like St. Charles, we can all develop a special love for pilgrimages and the veneration of relics, recognizing the power of these gifts in the promotion of faith, hope, and charity.

If you have interest in reading more about the life and work of St. Charles Borromeo, you've got your work cut out for you. It is a mystery that there are not more printed works on his life. Even if that remains a hurdle for you, the principal text for the life of St. Charles is the enormous work of Giovanni Pietro (John Peter) Guissano, *Life of St. Charles Borromeo*. This version is a detailed (as implied by its 600-plus pages) account of his life. In any case, his life is a pivotal one in the study of the Counter-Reformation, and any study involving the Council of Trent.

Prayer of St. Charles Borromeo

Almighty God, you have generously made known to human beings the mysteries of your life through Jesus Christ your Son in the Holy Spirit. Enlighten my mind to know these mysteries which your Church treasures and teaches. Move my heart to love them and my will to live in accord with them. Give me the ability to teach this Faith to others without pride, without ostentation, and without personal gain. Let me realize that I am simply your instrument for bringing others to the knowledge of the wonderful things you have done for all your creatures. Help me to be faithful to this task that you have entrusted to me. Amen.

Prayer to St. Charles Borromeo for a Happy Death

In the Name of the Most Holy Trinity, Father, Son and Holy Ghost, I, a poor, unhappy sinner, make this solemn declaration before thee, O beloved Angel, who has been given me as a protector by the Divine Majesty:

I desire to die in the Faith which the holy, Roman and apostolic Church adheres to and defends, in which all the saints of the new testament, have died. I pray thee, provide that I may not depart out of this life before the holy sacraments of that Church have been administered to me.

I pray that I may depart from this life under thy holy protection and guidance, and I beseech thee, therefore, to assist me at the hour of my death and to propitiate the eternal judge, whose Sacred Heart was inflamed with most ardent love for sinners upon the cross.

With my whole heart I long to be made a partaker of the merits of Jesus Christ and his holy mother Mary, thine exalted queen, and I pray thee, through the sufferings of Jesus on the cross, to mitigate the agonies of my death and to move the

Queen of Heaven to cast her loving glance upon me, a poor sinner, in that dreadful hour, for my sweetest consolation. O my dearest guardian angel! Let my soul be placed in thy charge, and when it has gone forth from the prison of this body, do thou deliver it into the hands of its Creator and Redeemer, that with thee and all the saints, it may gaze upon him in the bliss of heaven, love him perfectly and find its blessedness in him throughout eternity.

Amen.

About the Author

Mr. Shaun McAfee, O.P., is a convert to the Catholic faith. He is the author of *Filling Our Father's House,* the founder and editor of EpicPew.com, blogger at the *National Catholic Register,* and a contributor to many online Catholic resources. He holds a master's in dogmatic theology from Holy Apostles College and Seminary. Shaun and his family live in Vicenza, Italy.

Bibliographical Notes

Below is a bibliography listing each of the works, quotes, and major sources of information contained in this book.

Chapter 1: St. Francis de Sales

C.F. Kelley, "Letters to Persons in the World," *The Spiritual Maxims of St. Francis de Sales* (Kettering, OH: Angelico Press, 2014).

C.F. Kelley, "Spiritual Conferences," *The Spiritual Maxims of St. Francis de Sales* (Kettering, OH: Angelico Press, 2014).

Christopher Rengers, O.F.M. Cap., *The 35 Doctors of the Church revised edition* (Rockford, IL: Tan Books and Publishers, 2000).

Jean-Pierre Camus, *The Spirit of St. Francis de Sales*, (IndyPublish, 2004).

Louise Stacpoole-Kenny, *St. Francis de Sales: A Biography of the Gentle Saint* (Rockford, IL: Tan Books and Publishers, 2002).

"Saint Francois de Sales," *Letters of St. Francis de Sales*, Volume XIV of the Edition of Annecy, http://jesusmarie. free.fr/francois_de_sales_lettres_tome_4.html.

St. Francis de Sales, *Introduction to the Devout Life*, ed. John F. Thornton, Susan B. Varenne (New York, NY: Vintage Spiritual Classics, 2002).

St. Francis de Sales. *Letters to Persons in Religion*, ed. Henry Benedict Mackey (Read Books, accessed by Google Books, 2008).

St. Francis de Sales, *Treatise on the Love of God*, ed. Bernard Bangley (Brewster, MA: Paraclete Press, 2011).

Chapter 2: St. Ignatius of Loyola

Catholic Church "Declaration on Christian Education: Gravissimum Educationis." *Vatican II Documents*, (Vatican City: Libreria Editrice Vaticana, 2011).

Kevin O'Brien, *The Ignatian Adventure: Experiencing the Spiritual Exercises of St. Ignatius*, (Chicago, IL: Loyola Press, 2011).

St. Ignatius of Loyola, *The Autobiography of St. Ignatius of Loyola*, ed. J.F.X. O'Conor, S.J. (New York, NY: Benzinger Brothers, 1900).

St. Ignatius of Loyola, "Letter to Fr. Claude Jay on a Secret Mission of Charity (August 8, 1551)," *Selected Writings of St. Ignatius of Loyola*, ed. William J. Young, S.J., Georgetown University, http://www.library.georgetown.edu/woodstock/ignatius-letters.

St. Ignatius of Loyola. "Letter to Fr. Fulvio Androzzi on the Exercises as an Efficacious Means of Helping Souls (July 18, 1556)," *Selected Writings of St. Ignatius of Loyola*, ed. William J. Young, S.J., Georgetown University, http://www.library.georgetown.edu/woodstock/ignatius-letters.

St. Ignatius of Loyola, "Letter to the Fathers and Brothers Studying at Coimbra on Perfection (May 7, 1547)," *Selected Writings of St. Ignatius of Loyola*, ed. William J. Young, S.J., Georgetown University, http://www.library.georgetown.edu/woodstock/ignatius-letters.

St. Ignatius of Loyola. "Letter to Francisco de Borja, Duke of Grandía on Prayer and Penance (September 20, 1548)," *Selected Writings of St. Ignatius of Loyola*, ed. William J.

Young, S.J., Georgetown University, http://www.library.georgetown.edu/woodstock/ignatius-letters.

St. Ignatius of Loyola, "Letter to Br. Giovanni Battista on the Desire to Study (May 23, 1556)," *Selected Writings of St. Ignatius of Loyola*, ed. William J. Young, S.J., Georgetown University, http://www.library.georgetown.edu/woodstock/ignatius-letters.

St. Ignatius of Loyola, "Letter to Fr. Peter Canisius on the Society's Duty to Oppose Heresy (August 13, 1554)," *Selected Writings of St. Ignatius of Loyola*, ed. William J. Young, S.J., Georgetown University, http://www.library.georgetown.edu/woodstock/ignatius-letters.

St. Ignatius of Loyola, "Letter to Inés Pascual: A Letter of Spiritual Direction (December 6. 1524)," *Ignatius of Loyola: Spiritual Exercises and Selected Works*, ed. George E. Ganss, S.J. (Mahwah, NJ: Paulist Press, 1991).

St. Ignatius of Loyola, "Letter to Stefano Casanova on Moderation in Mortification (July 20, 1556)," *Selected Writings of St. Ignatius of Loyola*, ed. William J. Young, S.J., Georgetown University, http://www.library.georgetown.edu/woodstock/ignatius-letters.

St. Ignatius of Loyola, "Letter to Teresa Rejadell on Discernment of Spirits (June 18, 1536)," *Ignatius of Loyola: Spiritual Exercises and Selected Works*, ed. George E. Ganss, S.J. (Mahwah, NJ: Paulist Press, 1991).

St. Ignatius of Loyola, "Prayerful Thoughts," *Constitutions of the Society of Jesus: Monumenta Ignatiana: Epistolae et Instructiones*, ed. Joseph N. Tylenda, S.J., Georgetown University, http://www.library.georgetown.edu/woodstock/ignatius-letters/passages-26-50.

St. Ignatius of Loyola, *The Spiritual Exercises of St. Ignatius*, ed. Anthony Mottola (New York, NY: Image Books, 1964).

St. Thomas Aquinas, "Summa Theologiae," translated by Fathers of the English Dominican Province. (London, England: Burns Oates & Washbourne).

Chapter 3: St. Teresa of Ávila

Jodi Bilinkoff, *The Ávila of Saint Teresa: Religious Reform in a Sixteenth-Century City* (Ithaca, NY: Cornell University Press, 1989).

St. Teresa of Ávila, "The Book of Her Life," *The Collected Works of St. Teresa of Ávila Volume One*, ed. Kieran Kavanaugh, O.C.D., Otilio Rodriguez, O.C.D. (Washington, D.C.: Institute of Carmelite Studies, 1976).

St. Teresa of Ávila, *The Interior Castle*, ed. E. Allison Peers (Mineola, NY: Dover Publications, 1946).

St. Teresa of Ávila, *The Life of Saint Teresa of Ávila by Herself*, ed. J.M. Cohen (London, England: Penguin Group, 1957).

St. Teresa of Ávila, "Letter: Her mission in Carmel," *The Collected Works of St. Teresa of Ávila Volume One*, ed. Kieran Kavanaugh, O.C.D., Otilio Rodriguez, O.C.D. (Washington, D.C.: Institute of Carmelite Studies, 1976).

St. Teresa of Ávila, "Letter: Intellectual vision of a soul in grace and in sin (1571)," *The Collected Works of St. Teresa of Ávila Volume One*, ed. Kieran Kavanaugh, O.C.D., Otilio Rodriguez, O.C.D. (Washington, D.C.: Institute of Carmelite Studies, 1976).

St. Teresa of Ávila, "Letter: The vow of obedience to Fr. Gratian (April 1575)," *The Collected Works of St. Teresa of Ávila Volume One*, ed. Kieran Kavanaugh, O.C.D., Otilio Rodriguez, O.C.D. (Washington, D.C.: Institute of Carmelite Studies, 1976).

St. Teresa of Ávila, "Letter: True humility—put my counsels in writing (1572)," *The Collected Works of St. Teresa of Ávila Volume One*, ed. Kieran Kavanaugh, O.C.D., Otilio Rodriguez, O.C.D. (Washington, D.C.: Institute of Carmelite Studies, 1976).

St. Teresa of Ávila, "Letter: Revelation about the survival of her Carmel (Spring 1576)," *The Collected Works of St. Teresa of Ávila Volume One*, ed. Kieran Kavanaugh, O.C.D., Otilio Rodriguez, O.C.D. (Washington, D.C.: Institute of Carmelite Studies, 1976).

St. Teresa of Ávila, "On Making the Visitation," *The Collected Works of St. Teresa of Ávila Volume Three*, ed. Kieran Kavanaugh, O.C.D., Otilio Rodriguez, O.C.D. (Washington, D.C.: Institute of Carmelite Studies, 1985).

St. Teresa of Ávila, "Poem on the Efficacy of Patience," *The Collected Works of St. Teresa of Ávila Volume Three*, ed. Kieran Kavanaugh, O.C.D., Otilio Rodriguez, O.C.D. (Washington, D.C.: Institute of Carmelite Studies, 1985).

St. Teresa of Ávila, "The Foundations," *The Collected Works of St. Teresa of Ávila Volume Three*, ed. Kieran Kavanaugh, O.C.D., Otilio Rodriguez, O.C.D. (Washington, D.C.: Institute of Carmelite Studies, 1985).

Chapter 4: St. Robert Bellarmine

Catholic Church, "Decree on Ecumenism: Unitatis Redintegratio," In *Vatican II Documents* (Vatican City: Libreria Editrice Vaticana, 2011).

De Lamar Jensen, *Reformation Europe: Age of Reform and Revolution*, (Lexington, MA: D.C. Heath and Company, 1992).

James Brodrick, S.J., *Robert Bellarmine: Saint and Scholar* (Westminster, MD: The Newman Press, 1961).

James Hitchcock, *History of the Catholic Church* (San Francisco, CA: Ignatius Press, 2012).

Shaun McAfee, O.P., *St. Robert Bellarmine: For the Celebration of the Fiftieth Anniversary of St. Robert Bellarmine Catholic Church* (St. Louis, MO: En Route Books and Media, 2016).

St. Robert Bellarmine, *The Art of Dying Well*, ed. John Dalton (Manchester, NH: Sophia Institute Press, 2005).

St. Robert Bellarmine, *Steps of Ascension to God* (London, England: Aeterna Press, 2015).

T. A. Buckley, *The Canons and Decrees of the Council of Trent* (London, England: George Routledge and Co., 1851).

Chapter 5: St. Aloysius Gonzaga

Catholic Church "Declaration on Christian Education: Gravissimum Educationis." *Vatican II Documents*, (Vatican City: Libreria Editrice Vaticana, 2011).

Fr. Maurice Meschler, S.J., *St. Aloysius Gonzaga: Patron of Christian Youth* (Rockford, IL: TAN Books and Publishers, 1985).

J. F. X. O'Conor, *Life of St. Aloysius Gonzaga of the Society of Jesus* (New York, NY: St. Francis Xavier College, 1891).

Silas S. Henderson, *Saint Aloysius Gonzaga, S.J.: With an Undivided Heart* (San Francisco, CA: Ignatius Press, 2017).

Chapter 6: St. Pius V

Christopher Check, *Lepanto: The Battle that Saved the West* (speech and audio CD, San Diego, CA: Catholic Answers Press).

Diane Moczar, *Ten Dates Every Catholic Should Know: The Divine Surprises and Chastisements That Shaped the Church and Changed the World* (Manchester, NH: Sophia Institute Press, 2005).

James Hitchcock, *History of the Catholic Church* (San Francisco, CA: Ignatius Press, 2012).

Mark Greengrass, *The Longman Companion to the European Reformation C. 1500-1618* (Harlow, England: Longman Group UK, 1998).

St. Pius V, "Papal Bull on the Custom of the Roman Pontiffs: Consueverunt Romani Pontifices (September 17, 1569)," *Papal Encyclicals Online*, http://www.papalencyclicals.net/Pius05/p5consue.htm.

Pope Pius XI, "Encyclical on the Reconstruction of the Social Order: Quadragesimo Anno (May 15, 1931)," *The Papal Encyclicals: 1903–1939*, ed. Claudia Carlen (Ypsilanti, MI: The Pierian Press, 1990).

Robin Anderson, *Saint Pius V: A Brief Account of His Life, Times, Virtues and Miracles* (Rockford, IL: TAN Books and Publishers, 1978).

Williston Walker, *A History of the Christian Church* (New York, NY: Charles Scribner's Sons, 1918).

Chapter 7: St. Philip Neri

Antonio Gallonio, *Life of St. Philip Neri*, ed. Jerome Beltram (San Francisco, CA: Ignatius Press, 2005).

Frederick W. Faber, *Maxims and Sayings of St. Philip Neri*, ed. Thomas Richardson (Potosi, WI: St. Athanasius Press, 1847).

James Brodrick, S.J., *Robert Bellarmine: Saint and Scholar* (Westminster, MD: The Newman Press, 1961).

Fr. V. J. Matthews, *Saint Philip Neri: Apostle of Rome and Founder of the Congregation of the Oratory* (Charlotte, NC: TAN Books and Publishers, 1985).

Chapter 8: St. John of the Cross

"Prayers, Quips and Quotes; St. Philip Neri, Feast Day May 26," Catholic Faith Patron Saints, http://catholicfaith-patronsaints.com/prayers-quips-and-quotes-st-philip-neri-feast-day-may-26/.

Code of Canon Law: New English Translation (Washington, DC: Canon Law Society of America, 1998).

St. John of the Cross, "The Ascent of Mount Carmel," *John of the Cross: Selected Writings*, ed. Kieran Kavanaugh, O.C.D., Ernest E. Larkin, O. Carm. (Mahwah, NY: Paulist Press, 1987).

St. John of the Cross, *Dark Night of the Soul*, ed. E. Allison Peers (Overland Park: Digireads, from the critical edition of P. Silverio de Santa Teresa to the Discalced Carmelites of the Castile).

Richard P. Hardy, *St. John of the Cross: Man and Mystic* (Boston, MA: Pauline Books and Media, 2004).

St. Teresa of Ávila, "The Foundations," *The Collected Works of St. Teresa of Ávila Volume Three*, ed. Kieran Kavanaugh, O.C.D., Otilio Rodriguez, O.C.D. (Washington, D.C.: Institute of Carmelite Studies, 1985).

Chapter 9: St. Jane Frances de Chantal

Emily Bowles, *The Life of St. Jane Frances Frémyot de Chantal* (London, England: Burns and Oates, 1874).

Kathryn Hermes, *A Simple Life: Wisdom from Jane Frances de Chantal* (Boston, MA: Pauline Books and Media, 2011).

St. Jane Frances de Chantal, "Letter to Commandeur de Sillery—Noel Brulart (1633)," *Francis de Sales, Jane de Chantal: Letters of Spiritual Direction*, ed. John Farina, Peronne Marie Thibert, V.H.M. (Mahwah, NY: Paulist Press, 1988).

St. Jane Frances de Chantal, "Letters to the Archbishop of Bourges—Andre Frémyot (1625)," *Francis de Sales, Jane de Chantal: Letters of Spiritual Direction*, ed. John Farina, Peronne Marie Thibert, V.H.M. (Mahwah, NY: Paulist Press, 1988).

St. Jane Frances de Chantal, "Letter to Mother Anne Catherine de Beaumont, Superior of the First Visitation Monastery of Paris (1626)," *Selected Letters of Saint Jane Frances de Chantal*, ed. Sisters of the Visitation (London, England: Aeterna Press, 2015).

St. Jane Frances de Chantal, "Letters to Sr. Marie Aimee de Blonay, Mistress of Novices at Lyons (1616)," *Selected Letters of Saint Jane Frances de Chantal*, ed. Sisters of the Visitation (London, England: Aeterna Press, 2015).

St. Jane Frances de Chantal, "Letter to St. Vincent de Paul (1627)," *Selected Letters of Saint Jane Frances de Chantal*, ed. Sisters of the Visitation (London, England: Aeterna Press, 2015).

"Saints and Theology of the Heart," *Saint Jane Frances de Chantal: Co-Founder of the Visitation Order*, Pierced Hearts, https://www.piercedhearts.org/theology_heart/life_saints/jane_chantal.htm.

St. Thomas Aquinas, "Summa Theologiae," translated by Fathers of the English Dominican Province. (London, England: Burns Oates & Washbourne).

Chapter 10: St. Charles Borromeo

Code of Canon Law: New English Translation (Washington, D.C.: Canon Law Society of America, 1998).

John Calvin, *A Treatise on Relics*, ed. Count Valerian Krasinski (Edinburgh, Scotland: Johnson, Hunter & Co., 1870), accessed online at http://www.gutenberg.org/files/32136/32136-h/32136-h.html.

John Peter Giussano, *Life of Saint Charles Borromeo* (London, England: Burns and Oates, 1884).

Fabiola Giancotti, *Saint Charles Borromeo: Aphorisms (1561-1584)* (Italy: Il Club di Milano, 2012).

James Hitchcock, *History of the Catholic Church* (San Francisco, CA: Ignatius Press, 2012).

"Letter of the Smyrnaeans: The Martyrdom of Polycarp," New Advent: Church Fathers, http://www.newadvent.org/fathers/0102.htm.

Mark Greengrass, *The Longman Companion to the European Reformation C. 1500-1618* (Harlow, England: Longman Group UK, 1998).

Ray E. Atwood, *Masters of Preaching: The Most Poignant and Powerful Homilists in Church History,* quoting St. Charles Borromeo "Acta Ecclesiae Mediolanensis, Mediolani (1599)" (Lanham, MD: Hamilton Books, 2012).

St. Thomas Aquinas, *Summa Theologiae,* translated by Fathers of the English Dominican Province. (London, England: Burns Oates & Washbourne).

Endnotes

1. Louise Stacpoole-Kenny, *St. Francis de Sales: A Biography of the Gentle Saint*, p. 240.
2. *St. Francis de Sales*, p. 240-241.
3. Ibid., p. 28.
4. St. Francis de Sales. *Letters to Persons in the World*, part IV, section 53.
5. Jean-Pierre Camus, *The Spirit of St. Francis de Sales*, Book, part II, section 1.
6. Francis de Sales, *Introduction to the Devout Life*, part III, section 8.
7. *The Spirit of St. Francis de Sales*, part VII, section 9.
8. Ibid., part II, section 13.
9. *Introduction to the Devout Life*, part 3, section 30.
10. *Letters to Persons in the World*, part III, section 11.
11. *St. Francis de Sales*, p. 63.
12. Ibid., p. 232.
13. *The Spirit of St. Francis de Sales*, part XX, section 2.
14. *Introduction to the Devout Life*, part III, section 8.
15. *Letters to Persons in Religion*, part I, section 2.
16. *The Spirit of St. Francis de Sales, part* VII, section 2.
17. *Introduction to the Devout Life*, part I, section 3.
18. Ibid., part II, section 16.
19. St. Francis de Sales. *Treatise on the Love of God*, part VIII, section 11.
20. *Letters to Persons in Religion*, part V, section 5.

21. Fr. Christopher Rengers, *The 35 Doctors of the* Church, loc. 11094.

22. St. Ignatius of Loyola, *Autobiography of St. Ignatius of Loyola*, p. 19-21.

23. Kevin O'Brien, *The Ignatian Adventure: Experiencing the Spiritual Exercises of St. Ignatius*, p. 101.

24. *Autobiography*, p. 19.

25. Ibid., p. 105.

26. St. Ignatius of Loyola, *The Spiritual Exercises*, p. 47.

27. *Autobiography*, p. 111.

28. St. Ignatius of Loyola, *Letter to Fr. Claude Jay on a Secret Mission of Charity*.

29. *Letter to Fr. Claude Jay on a Secret Mission of Charity*.

30. Ibid.

31. *Letter to Fr. Peter Canisius on the Society's Duty to Oppose Heresy*.

32. Ibid.

33. Ibid.

34. St. Ignatius of Loyola, *Letter to Sr. Teresa Rejadell on Discernment of Spirits*.

35. *The Spiritual Exercises, annotations*.

36. St. Ignatius of Loyola, *Letter to Inés Pascual: A Letter of Spiritual Direction*.

37. *Autobiography*, p. 26.

38. St. Ignatius of Loyola, *Constitutions of the Society of Jesus*, no. 35.

39. *Summa Theologiae*, (II/II:82:2).

40. St. Ignatius of Loyola, *Letter to the Fathers and Brothers Studying at Coimbra on Perfection*.

41. The *Navarre Bible* reads: "Therefore, the apostle points out, the ascetical effort which every person must keep on making in this life includes physical mortification and self-control. Helped by God's grace and confident

of his mercy, a Christian who makes this effort will be able to say as St. Paul did at the end of his life, "there is laid up for me a crown of righteousness which the Lord, the righteous judge, will award to me on that day."

42. The Navarre Bible clarifies the allusion to mortification here, and in Matt. 5:30.

43. More on penances and mortifications is covered in detail in Chapter 5.

44. St. Ignatius of Loyola, *Letter to Stefano Casanova on Moderation in Mortification.*

45. St. Ignatius of Loyola, *Letter to Francisco de Borja, Duke of Grandía on Prayer and Penance.*

46. Ibid.

47. There is much more information on fasting in the Chapter about St. Aloysius Gonzaga.

48. *Letter to Francisco de Borja, Duke of Grandía on Prayer and Penance.*

49. *Letter to the Fathers and Brothers Studying at Coimbra.*

50. St. Ignatius of Loyola, *Letter to Fr. Fulvio Androzzi on the Exercises as an Efficacious Means of Helping Souls.*

51. St. Teresa of Ávila, *Letter: The vow of obedience to Fr. Gratian*, p. 405.

52. Ibid.

53. St. Teresa of Ávila, *The Foundations*, p. 64.

54. *Life of St. Charles Borromeo*, p. 574-577.

55. St. Teresa of Ávila, *The Book of Her Life*, p. 55.

56. St. Teresa of Ávila, *On Making the Visitation*, p. 337.

57. St. Teresa of Ávila, *Letter: Her mission in Carmel*, p. 401.

58. St. Teresa of Ávila, *The Book of Her Life*, p. 65.

59. St. Teresa of Ávila, *Letter: True humility—Put my counsels in writing*, p. 397.

60. St. Teresa of Ávila, *The Interior Castle*, p. 17.

61. Ibid., p. 16.

62. Ibid., p. 18.
63. Ibid.
64. Ibid., p. 28.
65. Ibid., p. 32.
66. St. Teresa of Ávila, *Letter: Intellectual vision of a soul in grace and in sin*, p. 394.
67. *The Interior Castle*, p. 37.
68. St. Teresa of Ávila, *The Life of Saint Teresa of Ávila by Herself*, p. 62–63.
69. *The Book of Her Life*, p. 96.
70. Ibid., p. 97.
71. *The Interior Castle*, p. 19.
72. *The Book of Her Life*, p. 98.
73. Ibid., p. 96.
74. Ibid., p. 140.
75. *The Interior Castle*, p. 40.
76. *The Book of Her Life*, p. 114.
77. *The Book of Her Life*, 129–130.
78. St. Teresa of Ávila, *Poem on the Efficacy of Patience*, p. 386.
79. Jodi Bilinkoff, *Ávila of Saint Teresa: Religious Reform in a Sixteenth Century Spain*, p. 151.
80. *Poem on the Efficacy of Patience*, p. 386.
81. T. A. Buckley, *The Canons and Decrees of the Council of Trent*, p. 19.
82. James Hitchcock, *History of the Catholic Church*, p. 263.
83. James Brodrick, *Robert Bellarmine: Saint and Scholar*, p. 156.
84. Bellarmine was the frontrunner to be elected pope in 1604, but let all the cardinals know that he did not want the duty. A month later when the newly elected pope Leo XI died, much like his uncle, Bellarmine was once again the front-runner. He said, "If picking up a straw from the ground would make me pope, the

straw would remain where it was." *Robert Bellarmine*, p. 238-245.

85. *Robert Bellarmine*, p. 70.
86. Ibid., p. 74.
87. St. Robert Bellarmine, *The Art of Dying Well*, p. 135.
88. *The Art of Dying Well*, p. 38.
89. Ibid., p. 38.
90. Ibid., p. 38.
91. *Apostolicam Actuositatem*, 2.
92. *The Art of Dying Well*, p. 37.
93. *Robert Bellarmine*, p. 33.
94. Ibid., p. 33.
95. Ibid., p. 33.
96. St. Robert Bellarmine, *Steps of Ascension to God*, loc. 2329.
97. *Robert Bellarmine*, p. 34.
98. Ibid., p. 53.
99. Silas S. Henderson, *Saint Aloysius Gonzaga, S.J.: With an Undivided Heart*, p. 182-184.
100. J. F. X. O'Conor, *Life of St. Aloysius Gonzaga of the Society of Jesus*, xii.
101. See Bishop Olmsted of Phoenix's exhortation, *Into the Breach*, available at IntotheBreach.org.
102. *Gravissimum Educationis*, 3.
103. Silas S. Henderson, *Saint Aloysius Gonzaga: With an Undivided Heart*, p. 79.
104. *Saint Aloysius Gonzaga: With an Undivided Heart*, p. 221.
105. *Life of St. Aloysius Gonzaga*, p. 106.
106. Ibid., p. 126.
107. In fact, his first spiritual director in Rome, the great Fr. Claudius Aquaviva had him wear a wooden frame on his neck and shoulders to keep his head up in order to share his wonderful smile with others. A poignant

reminder of his desire for humility and custody of the senses.

108. *Life of St. Aloysius Gonzaga*, p. 110.

109. Ibid., p. 125.

110. *Saint Aloysius Gonzaga: With an Undivided Heart*, p. 173.

111. *Life of St. Aloysius Gonzaga*, p. 177.

112. Ibid., p. 175.

113. Diane Moczar, *Ten Dates Every Catholic Should Know*, p. 131.

114. Mark Greengrass, *The Longman Companion to the European Reformation C. 1500-1618*, p. 317.

115. Williston Walker, *A History of the Christian Church*, p. 378.

116. Pius V, Papal Bull *Consueverunt Romani Pontifices*, 1, 2.

117. *Ten Dates Every Catholic Should Know*, p. 130.

118. Robin Anderson, *Saint Pius V*, p. 67.

119. The most widely accepted tradition is that it was promoted by St. Dominic while preaching against the Albigensians, but had been a prayer in various forms prior to this.

120. Pius XI, *Quadragesimo Anno*, 79.

121. St. Philip Neri, *The Maxims and Sayings of St. Philip Neri*, p. 22.

122. "St. Philip Neri," catholicpatronsaints.com.

123. *The Maxims and Sayings of St. Philip Neri*, p. 54.

124. Ibid., p. 61.

125. *Life of St. Philip Neri*, p. 200-206.

126. Antonio Gallonio, *The Life of St. Philip Neri*, p. 207.

127. Ibid., p. 43.

128. Ibid., p. 53.

129. Ibid., p. 123

130. *The Maxims and Sayings of St. Philip Neri*, p. 10.

131. *Life of St. Philip Neri*, p. 247.

132. *The Maxims and Sayings of St. Philip Neri*, p. 22.
133. James Brodrick, *Robert Bellarmine: Saint and Scholar*, p. 49.
134. *The Maxims and Sayings of St. Philip Neri*, p. 32–33.
135. Ibid., p. 21.
136. Ibid., p. 36.
137. Ibid., p. 35.
138. *The Life of St. Philip Neri*, p. 192.
139. St. Teresa of Ávila, *The Foundations*.
140. St. John of the Cross, *Dark Night of the Soul*, ch. 2.
141. Ibid.
142. Ibid., ch. 3
143. Ibid.
144. Ibid., ch. 4.
145. Ibid., ch. 5.
146. Ibid., ch. 6.
147. Ibid.
148. Refer to Code of Canon Law, §916.
149. *Dark Night of the Soul*, ch.7.
150. Ibid., ch. 2.
151. Richard P. Hardy, *John of the Cross: Man and Mystic*, p. 72.
152. St. John of the Cross, *The Ascent of Mount Carmel*, Book 1, ch. 2.
153. Ibid., Book 1, ch. 4.
154. Ibid., Book 3, ch. 15.
155. Ibid.
156. Ibid.
157. Ibid., Book 3, ch. 17.
158. *John of the Cross: Man and Mystic*, p. 104.
159. St. Jane Frances de Chantal, *Letter to Noel Brulart*, p. 185.
160. St. Jane Frances de Chantal, *Letter to St. Vincent de Paul*, p. 181.

161. St. Jane Frances de Chantal, *Letter to Sr. Marie Aimee de Bonay*, p. 48.

162. *Saint Jane de Chantal: Co-Founder of the Visitation Order.*

163. *Letter to Noel Brulart.* p. 188.

164. Ibid., p. 188.

165. Ibid., p. 189.

166. At the time, the new religious order was still nameless!

167. *Letter to Noel Brulart*, p. 193.

168. Ibid., p. 194.

169. See *Summa Theologiae*, (I:3).

170. *Letter to Noel Brulart*, p. 191.

171. St. Jane Frances de Chantal, *Letter to the Archbishop of Bourges*, p. 202.

172. Ibid.

173. Kathryn Hermes, *A Simple Life: Wisdom from Jane Frances de Chantal*, loc. 181.

174. Ibid., p. 203.

175. Ibid.

176. St. Jane Frances de Chantal, *Letter to mother Anne Catherine de Beaumont, Superior of the First Visitation Monastery of Paris.* p. 147.

177. *Letter to the Archbishop of Bourges*, p. 201.

178. Ray E. Atwood, *Masters of Preaching: The Most Poignant and Powerful Homilists in Church History*, p. 215.

179. E.g., Job 20:12, 27:4; Ps. 5:9, 15:3; Prov. 12:18, 21:23.

180. *Acta Ecclesiae Mediolanensis*, p. 1177–1178.

181. Giovanni Pietro Giussano, *Life of St. Charles Borromeo*, p. 241.

182. *Ibid.*, p. 258–262.

183. *Ibid.*, p. 27.

184. John Calvin, *Treatise on Relics*, p. 239.

185. *Letter of the Smyrnaeans: The Martyrdom of Polycarp*, ch. 18.

186. For more information clarifying the difference between holy veneration and worship of saints, see the Catholic Answers tract *Saint Worship?* At http://www.catholic. com/tracts/saint-worship.

187. St. Thomas Aquinas, *Summa Theologiae*, (III:25:6).

188. *Summa Theologiae*, (III:25:5).

189. *Aphorisms*, loc. 225.

190. Mark Greengrass, *The Longman Companion to the European Reformation C. 1500-1618*, p. 288.